An Administrator's Guide
to Online Education

a volume in
The USDLA Book Series on Distance Learning

Series Editor:
John G. Flores, *United States Distance Learning Association*

The USDLA Book Series of Distance Learning

John G. Flores, Series Editor

Electronic Learning Communities (2003)
edited by Sorel Reisman

An Administrator's Guide to Online Education

by

Kaye Shelton
Dallas Baptist University

and

George Saltsman
Abilene Christian University

published in cooperation with the

United States Distance Learning Association

INFORMATION AGE
PUBLISHING

Greenwich, Connecticut • www.infoagepub.com

Library of Congress Cataloging-in-Publication Data

Shelton, Virginia Kaye.
  An administrator's guide to online education / by Kaye Shelton and
George Saltsman.
    p. cm. — (USDLA book series on distance learning)
  Includes bibliographical references and index.
  ISBN 1-59311-425-7 (hardcover : alk. paper) — ISBN 1-59311-424-9
(pbk. : alk. paper)
    1. Distance education—Planning. 2. Distance
education—Administration. 3. Internet in higher education.
4. Universities and colleges—Administration.
5. Universities and colleges—Computer networks.
I. Saltsman, George. II. Title. III. Series.
  LC5803.P5S44 2005
  371.3'58—dc22

                                            2005024494

Printed in the United States of America

CONTENTS

FOREWORD

There is a myth that abounds in academic institutions. That myth promotes the notion that online distance learning programs are easy to set up, require little to no planning, and cost almost no money to operate. With the growing popularity of online courses and programs and the desire to get a piece of this market share, we have seen numerous programs emerge that have not necessarily been well planned and that lack quality. Some have been literally "thrown together" quickly and with little forethought. Others have grown out of the "Lone Ranger" approach of faculty who wanted to experiment with the medium. The myth leads to a belief that all it takes to deliver online courses is access to a course management system and faculty who know how to use that system. Nothing could be further from the truth. What administrators of these programs do not know is that the absence of planning is visible—it is visible to students who enroll in the courses and programs; it is visible to faculty who teach there; it is discussed at conferences and on listservs devoted to online learning.

In our own previous writing, we talked about the importance of good planning for online programs as well as the importance of focusing on faculty training for effective course delivery. We advocated a comprehensive approach that includes all aspects of the learning experience. As students seek out online programs and courses, they look for well-planned, high-quality programs with faculty who are well trained. This is often the key to determining student persistence online. Students have become knowledgeable consumers of distance learning and have learned how to judge quality. Given the level of competition in online learning today, when quality is not present, the students simply do not stick around.

Kaye Shelton and George Saltsman, in this timely and highly effective book, are debunking the myths surrounding the delivery of online courses and programs by discussing what it takes to plan, manage, and deliver these programs effectively. Through their own experience as distance learning program administrators as well as the experience of the numerous colleagues they have interviewed in the preparation of this book, they have created an essential text that anyone managing or thinking about managing an online program should read. Shelton and Saltsman cover the gamut from the theory behind online learning to essentials of leadership to planning and budgeting to working with faculty and students. As such, they have painted a complete picture of what needs to be done in order to create a program that will attract and retain both students and faculty as well as what will serve both groups in a high-quality manner.

Some might think that the time for such a book has passed given the proliferation of online programs. However, we feel that the time is exactly right for a book such as this one. It is never too late for administrators to examine what they are doing in the online arena and to focus on continuous quality improvement, which should be a goal for all programs. Shelton and Saltsman, through this comprehensive guide, are providing a beacon of light on what can be a dark path to the creation of an effective distance learning program. They answer the tough questions, address the thorny issues, and most importantly, eliminate the myths. Theirs is an important message that needs to be heard now.

Rena Palloff
Keith Pratt

PREFACE

Humans are explorers by nature. There is an innate trait inside each individual that seeks to find the unknown or look for the undiscovered. The same motivation that drove Ferdinand Magellan, Marco Polo, and Neil Armstrong drives us as educators. In the midst of the unbridled optimism of the 1990s, educators began exploring, both independently and collectively, the delivery of educational materials through a new medium called the World Wide Web. What these educational explorers discovered was not only a new educational paradigm, focused on student-centered learning, but a process that continues to revolutionize the way education is delivered across all disciplines and all modalities.

Constrained only by their dreams, online education pioneers tirelessly worked in pursuit of a single goal: to use the interactive capacity of the Internet to revolutionize distance education. They succeeded. In a recent survey in 2003, there were more than 1.9 million online students in American institutions of higher education and that number is expected to increase by almost 25% in 2004 (Allen & Seaman, 2004).

As online education enters its second decade, it is important to collectively examine online education's successes and failures. We must ask the questions: "What works?" and "What doesn't?" Understanding the answers to these questions allows academe to further improve the practice of online education and thus provide access to higher education for greater numbers of students more effectively. Prudent management requires such scrutiny.

Administration of online education is a complex task. There are dozens of areas that must be managed, each with their own unique challenges. Like pieces of a puzzle, these areas must be joined together carefully, ensuring that each piece is linked appropriately together with the next. The identification of the pieces is just the first step in solving the puzzle. Once the issues have been identified and understood, practice and policy should be put into place to systematically address those issues and further the chances for success.

Unlike most books regarding online education, this book is not about teaching; it is about effectively administering an online education program. Throughout the text, we provide case studies, examples, policies, and resources from actual institutions, which further enhance the value of this text. This book encompasses the issues and provides information on how to accomplish one specific task: successful online educational administration.

Grounded in existing distance education theory (chapter 1) and drawing from best practices, current research, and an extensive review of current literature, this book systematically identifies and discusses seven key issues that affect the practice of online education today:

Chapter 2. Leadership and Strategic Planning

- The critical need for upper-level administrative support
- Leadership roles and common strengths and weaknesses
- A strategic planning process for online education
- Three planning questions that every institution should address
- Additional goals and strategies employed by a successful institutions

Chapter 3. Policy and Operational Issues

- The need for policy in online education
- A policy analysis framework
- Blueprint for the Office of Online Education and a list of common job descriptions for the Director of Online Education
- Guidelines for creating an online education business plan including statistical data and policy examples
- Resources to estimate program cost, revenue, and growth

Chapter 4. Faculty Issues

- Strategies for faculty buy-in
- Policy to support and encourage online instruction
- Common faculty compensation models

- Addressing appropriate class size and faculty workload
- Incentives and perks provided for faculty to teach online
- Solutions for providing support for online faculty, both in online content creation and teaching

Chapter 5. Online Student Services

- The deconstructed campus
- How to construct a campus service assessment
- Specifically identifies the most common online student support offices

Chapter 6. Online Student Success

- Factors that affect student retention
- Ways to pre-assess online student success traits
- Technical assessments and orientation courses

Chapter 7. Technology and the Courseware Management System

- Three ways to support the technical infrastructure for online education
- Explanation of CMS features
- Discussion of commercial versus open source CMS products
- Overview of essential technology and suggested methods for supporting that technology
- Tools commonly used to support learning
- Learning object standards and the Sakai Project

Chapter 8. Marketing the Online Program

- Basic marketing strategies for the online program
- The need to market to both internal and external audiences
- The online education marketing mix
- Resources and guidelines for marketing the online program

Unfortunately, there is no single one-size-fits-all practice for online education. Each institution is unique, with is own mission, culture, and personality. Practitioners at each institution must weigh the range of options and competing practices against their institution's specific values and culture to select or adapt the most appropriate approach for their situation. This book respects the diversity of individual needs and, where possible, offers alternative approaches and different viewpoints as a resource to the online education team.

This book makes several basic assumptions. The material in this book is intended for traditional, nonprofit, brick-and-mortar institutions that have been offering courses in traditional classrooms for some length of time. We assume that the online education program is not completely self-sufficient. Most programs rely, at least partly, on some established centralized support services, such as the library, bursar's office, and so on. Finally, we assume that resistance to change is a constant. If you happen to be in an organization that embraces change easily, then (1) some of this text may not apply to you, and (2) you are exceptionally lucky!

ACKNOWLEDGMENTS

We would like to gratefully acknowledge many people for their unwavering support with this project. We gained so much from our colleagues, friends, peers, and coworkers. Thanks to all of you, who have in one way or another contributed to and shared your work in online education. We have drawn upon that knowledge often, not only in the creation of this book, but in our everyday work. Thank you to all of the online education administrators and staff who contributed to the interviews and case studies. The vision for this book was based on the sharing of your successes and struggles. It was your selfless contributions that made this book a reality.

- To our institutions, Dallas Baptist University and Abilene Christian University, thank you for allowing us the freedom to create and dream with this new method of teaching and learning. Thank you for not being afraid to step out and teach students in a new way while maintaining a high standard of academic quality.
- Dr. Rena Palloff and Dr. Keith Pratt, thank you for believing we had a story to tell. Your encouragement and support was the reason this project began.
- Sandee Smith, we are deeply indebted to you for the time you spent proofing our initial pages and for your refreshing encouragement throughout the process, we appreciate you!
- Jason Jones, thank you for your help, research, writing, and strategic insight into the marketing chapter. Your creative contributions were invaluable as well as enlightening and truly offer remarkable expertise for marketing an online program.

- Dr. Dave Arnott, thank you for that intensive but very helpful seminar in "How to Write a Book and Get it Published." Your words of wisdom were inspirational for beginning this project and your encouragement throughout the project was vital.
- Dr. Chip Ricketts, thank you for your guidance and direction in the marketing content that is so very important to the success of the online program.
- Dr. Bill Rankin, thank you for rescuing us from despair with your invaluable advice. We owe you whatever is left of our sanity.
- Randy Byers, thank you for the initial research you provided in those early days of the project.
- Finally, and most importantly, thank you, Lord, for giving us the opportunity of a lifetime.

From Kaye to:

- My husband, Rick, and sons, TJ, Matthew, and Nathan, thank you for allowing me the time for this project. Your unwavering support sustained me and I love each of you very much.
- Dr. Gary Cook, thank you for your vision, support, and guidance in creating a very successful model for a quality online education program that inspired this book. Your wisdom, knowledge, and faith were like the mustard seed; we hope it spreads throughout all of higher education.
- Dr. Gail Linam, my mentor and dear friend, thank you for your unwavering belief in not only me but my leadership of the DBU Online program.
- Dawn Evans, thanks for listening to all of my complaining and being a sounding board when I lost track.
- Dr. Mark Mortensen, thank you for encouraging me to go beyond the surface in the research. Your challenge was just what I needed in my quest for excellence.
- DBU Online Education team, thank you for your ongoing support during this project, we are a great team!

From George to:

- My wife Kristen and daughter Carrie Ann, thanks for all that you have done to support me. Your encouragement and love are, above all, appreciated and cherished.
- Dr. KB Massingill, Dr. Carol Williams, Dr. Dwayne VanRheenen, and Dr. Gary Tucker, thank you for the opportunity to be involved

with such a great organization. Thank you for your leadership, advice, and example.

- My family, thanks for the wonderful examples you have provided for me.
- The dozens of teachers and coaches, who, throughout my life, have pushed me to excel in whatever task I undertook and demanded nothing less than perfection.

ABOUT THE AUTHORS

Kaye Shelton, is the director of online education and assistant professor of adult education for Dallas Baptist University. She was also employed as the instructional program manager for distance learning at Florida Community College at Jacksonville–Virtual College. Ms. Shelton is a certified online instructor, teaching online since 1999, and also practices as an online education consultant. Her education includes a BAS in management of information systems, an MS in education emphasizing online teaching and learning, and she is currently pursuing a doctorate in educational computing. Ms. Shelton has published and presented on the subject of online education and has served as an advisor regarding online education programs for many peer institutions.

George Saltsman, is the director of educational technology for the Adams Center of Teaching Excellence at Abilene Christian University and serves as an adjunct part-time instructor for the Department of Journalism and Mass Communications. His education includes a BS in computer science and an MS in organizational and human resource development. Mr. Saltsman has managed ACU's distance education efforts for over 8 years, helping establish the initial strategic planning documents and the first online courses. He has published and presented on the subjects of online education and educational technology.

CHAPTER 1

INTRODUCTION TO
ONLINE EDUCATION

There are many ways of going forward, but only one way of standing still.
—Franklin D. Roosevelt

What a difference a few years make! Believe it or not, in 1990, the U.S. Department of Labor (1999) reported that only 15% of U.S. households owned a computer. The Internet had just barely 300,000 host computers and the World Wide Web protocol would still not be invented for another year (Computer History Museum, 2004). Now, fast-forward to today. Who could then have imagined a world in which musicians compose music without instruments, artists paint without brushes, or teachers teach without classrooms? Because of the pervasiveness of technology, the very nature of the workplace has changed within our generation.

Just as the computer revolutionized the workplace, the digital revolution is having a similar impact on higher education. We see computers throughout academe and many face-to-face courses now have online components. Complaints from faculty about the speed of their computers have almost replaced complaints about office size. Even those of us who were around long before the age of the personal computer find ourselves searching the Internet first before venturing into the library.

As the need for lifelong learning in an increasingly complex information-based society has brought distance education new acclaim (Garrison, 2000), online education has provided the opportunity to reach that soci-

---

An Administrator's Guide to Online Education, 1–8
Copyright © 2005 by Information Age Publishing
All rights of reproduction in any form reserved.

ety with an efficacy unmatched in education's history. Forward-looking institutions, recognizing the changing landscape of higher education and the potential of the Internet as a communication tool, originated the first online courses. These innovative courses, and the pedagogical evolution that followed, consequently challenged long-held beliefs and forced academe to reexamine many long-used practices.

What has now been termed as *online education* has subsequently created a market that is increasing at a remarkable rate and is responsible for a major growth segment in the education industry (Martz, Reddy, & Sangermano, 2004). A 2002 survey indicates more than 1.6 million students took at least one online course; 578,000 of those students took all of their courses online; and 81% of all institutions offer at least one online course (Allen & Seaman, 2003). In the same year, it was reported that distance education programs and online education was growing more than 40% annually (Eduventures, 2002). That trend was confirmed by more recent statistics showing the number of students approaching 2 million in 2003 (Allen & Seaman, 2004). Regardless of the actual numbers, the creation of a new, student-centered form of technology-enhanced education in such a short time is nothing less than remarkable.

What academe is experiencing today is only the beginning of what may be the largest paradigm shift in education during our lifetimes (Maddux, Ewing-Taylor, & Johnson, 2002). This changing paradigm is producing both excitement and renewed enthusiasm in learner-centered pedagogy, while simultaneously transforming the institution.

Although it was challenging, pioneering institutions of higher education adapted long-standing institutional practices to meet the needs of this new paradigm. They quickly found that changing traditional processes within the established institutional infrastructure requires knowledge, skill, institutional leadership, and a lot of old-fashioned hard work. Because of their efforts, however, online education now has the potential to surpass all other modes of distance education in terms of enrollment.

In order to establish a framework for understanding online education, the remainder of this chapter provides a formal definition of online education and discusses distance education theory as it relates to online education. It also provides rationale for institutions and presents the most prevalent issues in online education today.

WHAT EXACTLY IS ONLINE EDUCATION?

Online education, informally defined as the delivery of education using computers and the Internet, is a mode for instructional methodology in distance education. Distance education is not new to higher education, yet the methods of delivery are changing (Saunders, 2002). Simonson, Smaldino, Albright, and Zvacek (2003) believe this change "is one of the most dramatic of the recent technology-based innovations influencing education" (p. 5). Distance education was reported to have begun in England in 1840 (Rumble, 2001; Simonson et al., 2003) and has existed in the United States since 1873 (Simonson et al., 2003; Sumner, 2000; Watkins, 1991). In the last 30 years, various modes of distance education delivery such as satellite transmission, audio, and two-way video have emerged in response to societal expectations and introductions of technology. These modes of instruction, considered nontraditional, have now become an accepted form of instruction at many institutions (Gunawardena & McIsaac, 2003). Online education is now the newest mode to undergo acceptance.

Creating a formal definition for distance education is important, not only to describe what distance education is but to help define what it is not. Desmond Keegan (1996) offered the following as a formal definition of distance education:

- The quasi-permanent separation of teacher and learner throughout the length of the learning process (this distinguishes it from conventional face-to-face education);
- The influence of an educational organization both in the planning and preparation of learning materials and in the provision of student support services (this distinguishes it from private study and teach-yourself programs);
- The use of technical media—print, audio, video or computer—to unite teacher and learner and carry the content of the course;
- The provision of two-way communication so that the student may benefit from or even initiate dialogue (this distinguishes it from other uses of technology in education); and
- The quasi-permanent absence of the learning group throughout the length of the learning process so that people are usually taught as individuals rather than in groups, with the possibility of occasional meetings, either face-to-face or by electronic means, for both didactic and socialization purposes. (p. 50)[1]

A working definition that is widely accepted as a formal definition of distance education is adapted from the definition proposed by the United States regional accreditation associations. It is:

Distance education is defined, for the purposes of accreditation review, as a formal educational process in which the majority of the instruction occurs when student and instructor are not in the same place. Instruction may be

Table 1.1.   Distance Learning Definition Resource

For a more detailed explanation of the terms used to describe distance learning, see *Distance Learning: A Systems View: An Assessment and Review of the Literature* by Rosemary Ruhig DuMont (2002) available at: http://www.kent.edu/rcet/proposals/loader.cfm?url=/commonspot/security/getfile.cfm&PageID=1538

synchronous or asynchronous. Distance education may employ correspondence study, or audio, video, or computer technologies. (The Commission on Colleges, 1997)[2]

For this book, we propose the formal definition of online education that follows Keegan's definition of distance education with the computer and Internet as the technical media, rather than print, audio, or video. This holds true since online education is simply another method of instruction within the larger field of distance education. Because of this close relationship, the phrases *online education*, *distance education*, *Web-based instruction*, *online learning*, *distance learning*, *distributed learning*, and, to some extent, *e-learning* are used interchangeably throughout this book.

DISTANCE EDUCATION THEORY

There is a general disregard for the use of theory in online education and distance education programs. Moore realized, "To many newcomer practitioners ... distance education is perceived as a brand new field rather than one with a long history having its own body of research and theory" (as cited in Berge & Schrum, 1998, p. 31). The disregard for theory creates replication of effort and duplication of error in the practice of online education. Distance education theories have much to offer to the administrator of an online program. In fact, Meyer (2002) concludes that much of the distance education theorists' efforts support online education.

In the practitioner's defense, distance education theory is still under development, with emerging concepts and overlapping constructs. The lack of a single or a recognized set of theories confuses both the discipline and the practitioner. Although distance education has been utilized as a mode of instruction at least as far back as 1840, Holmberg (1995) suggests it was largely "characterized by trial and error approaches with little consideration being given to a theoretical basis for decision making" (as cited in Simonson et al., 2003, p. 37). Keegan (1983) recognized early on that further development of distance education theory was needed. He recommends, "A firmly based theory of distance education will be one which can provide the touchstone against which decisions—political, financial, edu-

Table 1.2.   Distance Learning Theory Resources

- *Foundations of Distance Education, 3rd Edition* (1996) by Desmond Keegan.
- "Theory and Distance Education: A New Discussion" by Michael Simonson, Charles Schlosser, and Dan Hanson (1999) in the *American Journal of Distance Education, 13*(1).
- "Distance Education Theory, Methodology, and Epistemology: A Pragmatic Paradigm (2003) by Farhad Saba in *Handbook of Distance Education.*

cational, social—when they have to be taken, can be taken with confidence" (p. 3). Keegan concluded that well-developed theory "would replace the ad hoc response to a set of conditions that arises in some 'crisis' situation of problem solving, which normally characterizes this field of education" (p. 3).

It is our recommendation that the online education administrator should take the time to review the various theories of distance education to gain a critical perspective of their programs. Theories such as Wedemeyer's Theory of Independent Study, Holmberg's Theory of Interaction and Communication, and Simonson's Equivalency Theory all provide structure for improving program design. As the literature demonstrates, theorists created excellent frameworks for distance education that still apply to online education today. In online education, the basic concept of distance education is still valid; the teacher and learner are separated and the student is central to program development. Garrison (2000) suggests, "The challenge [now] is to provide theory that will explain and anticipate distance education practices for a broad range of emerging educational purposes and experiences" (p. 1). These theories continue to offer relevance as the technology brings us closer to the traditional classroom experience.

WHY ONLINE EDUCATION?

Any educational methodology must be justified as both a legitimate and worthwhile endeavor. Online education has found justification within higher education and is no longer experimental (Garrison & Anderson, 2003). There were many reasons that institutions began offering online education programs. Some reasons were valid; others were perhaps not as compelling. Online education has had more than its share of hype; however, real promise exists for institutions and students: increased access and flexibility.

During the days of the Internet gold rush, college administrators saw both the threat of increased competition from other online schools as well as opportunities of increased markets (Sachs, 1999). Futurists predicted the end of traditional higher education with such dire forecasts as "10% of existing public colleges and 50% of independent colleges will close in the next 25 years" (Dunn, 2000, p. 34). Management theorist Peter Drucker warned that "traditional universities as we know them will become a wasteland in the next 25 years" (as cited in Dunn, 2000, p. 34). Yet, at the same time, optimists were making equally broad predictions. The *New York Times* observed that many thought "students would flock to the Web by the tens of thousands, paying tuitions comparable to those charged in the bricks-and-mortarboard world" (Hafner, 2002, p. G1). Prior to that, Buikema and Ward (1999) wrote that distance education "increases enrollment, attracts more qualified students, increased retention rates and graduation rates, and increases prestige" (as cited in Matthews, 2002, p. 6). With these miraculous possibilities coupled with these gloomy predictions, there was little wonder that the promise of online education attracted more than just passing interest from college administrators.

Unfortunately, much of the early hype for e-learning coincided with equally inflated promises for Internet commerce. This blurred the real promise of online education, which is still increased access to education (Dillon & Cintrón, 1997; Finkelstein & Scholz, 2000; Matthews, 2002; Miller & King, 2003; Moore & Kearsley, 1996; Verduin & Clark, 1991). Fortunately, many in academe were able to see through the hype to the true value of online education. When the speculative bubble of dotcom-based stocks burst in 2000, the inflated justifications for following an eCommerce-based model to capitalize on the education market no longer held promise. Higher education, for the most part, followed a more constrained approach to online education than the failed dotcoms did to eCommerce. There were still highly publicized failures such as Columbia's Fathom, Temple Online, California Virtual University, and NYU Online (Easley, 2002). However, for many higher education institutions, online education was proving to be successful as an instructional modality (Berge & Schrum, 1998). It was also financially justifiable, as institutions realized a new source of revenue (Sumner, 2000) and reduced the need for new campus buildings (Matthews, 1999).

Institutions justify online education in several ways. Dixon (1996) observed three reasons colleges and universities offer distance education: to fulfill a mission of delivery to a large service area; to accommodate population growth by increasing enrollment without spending money on buildings and land; and to reach a wider student population by gathering more potential students who otherwise wouldn't be able to attend classes (as cited in Seehusen, 2000). More recently, Matthews (2002) suggests distance education for the traditional university can be designed as an extension to overcome problems of scarcity and exclusivity and to increase the campus structure. Finally, Berge and Schrum (1998) suggest justification in that "distance education often serves as a catalyst for the adoption of learner-centered approaches to instruction" (p. 5), which places more emphasis on the students' needs for flexible learning.

Students find justification in online education because it "overcomes geographical, temporal or psychological barriers to participation in education" (Verduin & Clark, 1991, p. 104). These students value "convenience, choice, and flexibility" (Johnson, 2003, p. 149) with scheduling, especially important for time-deficient adults (Berg, 2002). Of course, students also value the increased access to education (Hanna, 2003) and a broader choice of educational programs in which they can selectively participate.

ISSUES IN ONLINE EDUCATION

Much has been written recently regarding the issues that confront distance education. Implementation of an initiative as large as an online education program involves a significant segment of the institution's support staff and there are numerous issues that can impede successful implementation. Those issues require change throughout the institution. Unfortunately as Howard, Schenk, and Discenza (2004) recognize, "Universities are embracing distance education, yet most are not making the changes necessary to maximize the effectiveness and efficiency of online learning" (p. vi).

Oblinger and Kidwell (2000) acknowledge that "distance education represents the convergence of a host of issues for higher education" (p. 31). Institutions may have numerous issues such as lack of skills among personnel, organizational structures that are resistant to change, and culture that resists change (Kotter, 1996, as cited in Edmonds, 1999). Berge and Muilenburg (2000) developed a list of 64 barriers that were summarized from the literature, case studies, and surveys. From that list, Berge developed an instrument that was administered between 1999 and 2000 to over 2,500 individuals, which included support staff, teachers, managers, higher education administrators, and researchers. The results of the survey are too detailed for the scope of this book, but it is interesting to note that the large majority of the perceived "strongest barriers" are those in which administrators have either control or direct influence. This implies that many of the perceived barriers could be removed with appropriate action and insight from leadership within the institution itself. This raises the question: Why have those actions not been taken? What causes these barriers to remain in place at some institutions while similar barriers at other institutions were removed? We believe, as outlined in Chapter 2, the answer lies in the involvement of upper-level administration to empower management to remove the barriers once they have been identified.

The word "barrier," when used in this context, can have two meanings. Barriers are sometimes seen as roadblocks that stop the progress of online education in its tracks (such as lack of funding). In other cases, barriers are seen more as just impediments to successful implementation (such as competition with on-campus courses). The latter implies that online education can succeed despite the "barrier," but perhaps not as quickly or easily as it might have otherwise.

It is clear from looking at the numerous schools involved in online education that many have found a way around the roadblocks, as over 81% of all institutions have offered at least one fully online course (Allen & Seaman, 2003). Perhaps it is just semantics, but we perfer the use of the word "issues" rather than "barriers" to describe the impediments to program growth and success. There are textbook examples of successful online education programs, yet every program still has its issues—problems or areas of concern that must be solved in order to sustain the growth, quality, or its existence over the long term. Therefore, this book's structure focuses on the major issues (rather than barriers) that are affecting online education today, provides discussion from the existing literature, and illustrates practices from successful institutions. These issues are summarized into the following categories:

> Leadership and Strategic Planning—Chapter 2
> Policy and Operational Issues—Chapter 3
> Faculty Issues—Chapter 4
> Online Student Services—Chapter 5
> Online Student Success—Chapter 6
> Technology and the Courseware Management System—Chapter 7
> Marketing the Online Program—Chapter 8

NOTES

1. From *Foundations of Distance Education* (3rd ed.), 1996, p. 50. Copyright 1996 by Taylor & Francis Group Ltd. Reprinted with permission.
2. Used with permission of The Commission on College: Southern Association of Colleges & Schools.

CHAPTER 2

LEADERSHIP AND STRATEGIC PLANNING

There is nothing more difficult to take in hand, more perilous to conduct,
or more uncertain in its success, than to take the lead in the
introduction of a new order of things.

—Niccolo Machiavelli

To write a bestselling business book, you only need to put the word "leadership" in the title—or at least that appears to be the case. While that might not be *completely* true, there is little doubt that leadership is a hot topic in today's business world and in academe too. Education needs strong leadership, and leaders are not always as abundant as the need. This chapter addresses the necessity for strong leadership in online education and provides in-depth information regarding the strategic planning process.

LEADERSHIP

A leader with institutional authority must champion the online program for it to reach its fullest potential. Upper-level administrative support is necessary to bring about the required organizational change within the institution. Leadership must be applied for online education to be successful due to the required strategic decisions (Kofahi & Srinivas, 2004).

An Administrator's Guide to Online Education, 9–30
Copyright © 2005 by Information Age Publishing
All rights of reproduction in any form reserved.

However, administrators are not always comfortable with the notion of online education. Perhaps it is because of its nebulous nature, or its non-traditional, decentralized student body, or maybe the administration's lack of vision for a different way of educating.

Online programs, in order to be integrated into the campus structure and truly accepted into academic culture, need a champion to communicate the possibilities and promote implementation. Haughey (2003) proposes "there are three aspects to the change process: the realization of the need for change; the mobilization of internal and external support for the change; and the actual implementation of the change and its integration into the ongoing operations of the organization" (p. 59). The first and third aspects can be achieved by faculty; it is the second aspect, the mobilization of the campus, that requires the institutional leader and administrative champion.

The Importance of Leadership

In comparison to the numerous volumes of materials regarding the teaching and learning aspects of online education, there is substantially less written on the subject of leadership. What is written, however, is strongly supportive of the need for top-level leadership. In fact, Berge (1998) confirms that "online teaching and learning will fail without strong administrative leadership to support the many changes necessary to fully implement online educational activities" (¶ 24).

Garrison and Anderson (2003) recognized during a process of change, leadership that anticipates the vision is necessary for successful transformation. They suggest leadership traits such as integrity and openness, fairness, honesty, and respect are required to fully integrate the online program into the institution. Dede (1993) and Beaudoin (2003) also urge for active leadership in the establishment of distance education programs. These characteristics and leadership values are necessary to move the program past organizational impasse (Prestera & Moller, 2001). The program's champion will have a significant effect on setting the tone toward the online program within the institution (Milheim, 2001). Beaudoin reminds us that "a university president or elected public official who endorses, articulates and facilitates distance education goals crafted by others can have a widespread impact" (pp. 519–520). This certainly does not mean the university president or other upper-level administrators must be involved in the daily routine of managing the online program; however, it does imply they must be personally invested in the success of the program. An administrative champion can be anyone with some institutional authority that would help to "redefine people's paradigms about what is possible" (Dede, 1993, p. 19) with online education and motivate the institution to action.

Fitzgerald (1998) recognized that either the introduction of, or changes in, technology creates a climate of confusion and apprehension (as cited in Marcus, 2004). Implementation of widescale institutional changes, such as the establishment of online education, requires a leader—a person who can motivate an entire institution with a vision. This leader must construct a vision and plan for accomplishing the vision that adequately transform that idea from a concept to reality. Beaudoin (2003) identifies leadership in distance education as "a set of attitudes and behaviors that create conditions for innovative change, that enable individuals and organizations to share a vision and move in its direction, and that contribute to the management and operationalization of ideas" (p. 519). That vision must be strong enough to empower those individuals in the institution to work toward achievement. Dede (1993) further suggests that "creating and conveying technological visions powerful enough to displace traditional educational models is one of the most challenging aspects of leadership" (p. 24). This type of leadership, conveying a descriptive and empowering vision, assists the organization through a potentially chaotic time.

As for the importance of vision and leadership, U.S. President John F. Kennedy (1961) demonstrated one of the best examples when he stood in front of Congress and said: "I believe that this nation should commit itself to achieving the goal, before this decade is out, of landing a man on the moon and returning him safely to the earth." This statement galvanized Congress and the entire nation in support of a goal. What was then a struggling space program became the focus of an entire world. Fortunately, developing an online program is much less complicated than putting a man on the moon; however, it does require the same persistence and active leadership to make it a successful reality.

Leadership Roles

Marcus (2004) identified three roles for distance education leaders: a transformational leader, a situational leader, and a systemic leader. According to Beaudoin (2003), the transformational role in distance education is the most important as these leaders help stakeholders understand that new methods of teaching could no longer be adopted by just a few brave instructors. Marcus defines the transformational leader as one "helping stakeholders to realize the benefits of distance education" (¶11) and the need for reshaping the institution. The situational leader is defined by Hershey and Blanchard (1977) as one who can assess the readiness of the organization or its stakeholders for change (as cited in Beaudoin, 2003). This leader is flexible enough to adapt to any situation. Finally, the systemic leader uses a holistic and universal approach, including relationship management, to lead change across the institution. Harmonizing these leadership styles is not easy, yet it is important for fully realizing the vision of the online program.

The emphasis on administrative leadership is not to discount or minimize the grassroots approach of individual faculty members and persistent staff who believed in the promises of e-learning and struggled to bring forth the online education programs existing on many campuses today. In fact, good leadership is not practiced by only those in administrative roles (Beaudoin, 2003). Shared leadership provides opportunity for such approaches to reach mainstream acceptance in the institution. In fact, we agree with Berge and Schrum (1998) that it is a combination of top-down leadership alongside bottom-up support that creates the most success. Champions of changes must rely upon agents of change to bring the vision to fruition. It is within the role of change agent that faculty and staff may find their most productive role in bringing online education into the mainstream within their organization.

Dede (1993) urges that a good leader encourages and empowers individuals to further a vision, creating an organization that is open to innovation. He emphasizes that "real leaders discourage followers, instead encouraging use of their visions as a foundation for other, and better insights. True solutions to problems are always based on ideas from multiple perspectives; no individual, however capable, can incorporate the full range of knowledge and experience needed to invent an educational system that fulfills the needs of a diverse community" (p. 27). The lack of leadership stifles the growth of otherwise well-intentioned programs.

Consider the following example: one institution we interviewed had a particularly difficult time adapting their existing campus infrastructure to accept the newly created online education program. While this institution was a technological leader among its peers, its attempt in starting an online program was met with frustration. Necessary logins to a campuswide courseware management system (CMS) were automatically created and widely used among traditional students. The problem began when distance education students began to enroll in the university's first fully online course. An automated process for the creation of student computer accounts was tied to an on-campus check-in requirement. As distance students enrolled in courses, they quickly discovered they could not obtain usernames and passwords without visiting the campus in person.

The school scrambled the first few weeks of the semester trying to identify online students who did not have CMS accounts. After panicked efforts, the accounts were eventually created without the on-campus check-in; however, university policy prevented the emailing of passwords. The Information Technology staff, citing larger security concerns, declined to modify the policy. The only option was to call the student with the password or wait for postal mail to reach the student. Some students took a day off from work, drove in, and obtained their accounts, while other students simply dropped the program and enrolled elsewhere.

The account issue was not an easy one to solve. It took rewriting customized computer programs and altering campuswide policies and procedures. This type of problem is not unique to online education programs in the startup phase. Campus infrastructure that has existed for years requires reengineering in order to accommodate online students. What made this problem significant for the online program was the lack of support from upper administration, as program leadership was fractured and vague. When the request to redesign the account creation process was received, it was given low priority and pushed aside for what was perceived as larger, more institutionally important requests. When the request to modify the policy was received, it was also denied. Unfortunately, without an upper-level administrator to push for an immediate change, the next semester met with much the same frustration.

In this example, the user account problem was eventually corrected, but the online program still struggles with similar issues and has yet to become successful. Time, money, and effort were lost. But more importantly, students were frustrated, faculty lost respect for the program, and the school's institutional reputation was affected. The initiative lacked the necessary administrative support to impel the program past the roadblocks for success.

STRATEGIC PLANNING

Great leadership involves careful and effective communication to the organization. The communication of expectations, desires, and goals to members of the organization is what enables dreams to become reality. Bates (2000) observes that "it is difficult enough for an individual to identify and describe accurately a personal vision for the future; it is even more difficult to create one for an organization as complex and diverse as a large research university" (p. 44). A strategic planning process provides that vision and communication to the organization. According to Noonan (2003), successful leaders cannot realize goals without other members of the organization. It is these people who must work diligently toward a shared vision and attempt to achieve a common goal. If the institution is to be successful at implementing and sustaining an initiative like online education, a strategic plan for should be developed. In reality, though, it may be as Fulkerth

(1999) suggests, that many distance education projects are integrated into the strategic plan once they have proven to be successful.

The literature emphasizes the importance of strategic planning in distance education. Care and Scanlan (2001) urge that "senior administrators in universities and colleges must invest in a strategic plan for distance education. Management must provide leadership in developing this plan for the institution as a whole. Unit administrators (Deans, Directors, Department Heads) can then adopt the strategic directions that best suit their needs" (¶22). Buchanan (2002) agrees, advising "institutions cannot jump into distance education without forethought and careful planning" (p. 143); she asserts that "institutions must create solid and strategic plans for meeting the needs of distance students" (p. 143). Finally, Moore and Kearsley (1996) determine strategic planning as one of the more critical phases for successful distance education. With the importance of strategic planning evident, administrators are tasked with initiating and leading the strategic planning process.

Obviously, this process of strategic planning is much easier said than done, as management strategists Mintzberg, Quinn, and Voyer (1995) surmise "that the weakest link in any planning initiative is the creation and implementation of strategies and tactics" (p 407). Garrison (2000) agrees that "few have the conceptual understanding to create a strategic plan for adopting distance education methods congruent with their institutional values and goals" (p. 2). Therefore, it is easy to understand why this process may have been ignored in the earlier development of online education programs, as Prestera and Moller (2001) observed that in the rush to get courses online, it was easy to miss the planning phase.

However, even in institutions that are not currently working under a strategic plan, the planning process should still be performed. The process helps to discover inadequacies and allow for the realignment of priorities for the organization to reach its maximum potential. For those institutions that did complete the strategic planning process, care should be taken to revisit the plan on a periodic basis and effectively communicate the progress. Bates (2000) observes that "too often strategic plans are developed but poorly disseminated to staff, forgotten about after an intense period of developing them" (p. 55), which could lead to frustration and program inefficiency.

Creating the Strategic Plan

Creating a strategic plan for online education is a multistep process. It requires "research, planning and program design on many levels" (Boettcher, 2004b, p. 23). Strategic planning has been extensively researched for use in business, and recently, within distance education. As a result, there are several models that have been proposed for use in education and distance education, most notably Compora's (2003) Administrative Operative Model and Haché's (1998) Systemic Model. In addition, Berge and Schrum (1998) provide a discussion on leadership in strategic planning, and Garrison and Anderson (2003) and Boettcher (2004b) provide a list of required topics for a strategic plan. Finally, McCune (1986) offers a helpful guide to general strategic planning for educators and Watkins and Kaufman (2003) provide excellent suggestions for strategic planning within distance education.

In spite of these excellent resources, it appears that no single approach is widely practiced. We believe, like Evans (2003), what is important is "a good understanding of the institution's history, strengths, weaknesses, a clear assessment of the current circumstances, and a rational and careful analysis of what options are available for the future" (p. 37). Bates (2000) also recognizes that "most successful strategies are not totally planned in advance" (p. 210), but as long as the institution follows a clearly defined approach for role identification, resource allocation, and program evaluation, the plan has a good chance of succeeding.

Since institutions across the United States utilize various approaches, there is room to improvise a customized plan to fit the specific needs of an institution. Boettcher (2004b) suggests an institution's planning process begin with a vision and mission statement and then allow for information gathering throughout the institution. The process of building upon the institution's vision, core values, and mission statement provides direct support for the development of specific goals and objectives, defining the program scope, strategies, policies, and action plans based on a comprehensive needs assessment. Therefore, building on suggestions of Boettcher (2004b)and others, we suggest the following top-down model for strategic planning:

- Vision, Value, and Mission Statements
- Needs Assessment
- Goals and Objectives
- Strategies
- Policies and/or Action Plans

The process should be sequential, as each phase supports the next step in the list. Developing planning documents out of sequence could risk possible misalignment of actions with institutional core values and mission.

Ideally, these documents would be prepared up to a year before the program begins (Buchanan, 2002). However, many institutions have already begun to offer online courses, and these documents have yet to be created;

or if they have, they need to be reexamined. For those institutions that have not begun to offer online courses, strategic planning can still occur but in a shorter time frame, as Buchanan (2002) recognizes that "most institutions will not have a year of planning and preparation" (p. 151).

Developing a Vision Statement

It is debatable which should be developed first, the mission statement or the vision statement. In many respects, these are interchangeable as they should complement each other. There are, however, key differences between a mission statement and a vision statement. Birnbaum (2004) explains that a vision statement not only points toward the future, but begins in the future since a vision is not able to exist in the present. A vision statement should be clear and concise while motivating, inspiring, and giving direction (C. Conner, personal communication, January 18, 2005).

A vision statement, by definition, needs only to be visionary, stating what the program wants to be in the future. But to be truly effective, it should paint a picture that is both vivid and compelling. An excellent example of a vision statement can be taken from Martin Luther King Jr.'s *I Have a Dream* speech. In this now historic speech, he offers a vibrant depiction of a future in which he dreams that his "four little children will

Table 2.1.   Virginia Polytechnic Institute and State University Institute for Distance and Distributed Learning Vision Statement for Distance Education

Virginia Tech will be a world-class leader in eLearning, transcending the barriers of time and place to offer new knowledge for a global community. In support of this vision, the Institute for Distance and Distributed Learning will:

- Employ a holistic approach to distance and distributed learning;
- Provide eLearning knowledge and expertise to university leadership;
- Encourage a learner-centered approach to education;
- Provide accessible and scalable teaching and learning resources and support services for students, faculty, and staff;
- Ensure that distance learning efforts are committed to quality and continuous improvement and meet new learner requirements and expectations;
- Actively participate in and support teaching, research, and outreach;
- Be an adaptive learning organization that recognizes excellence and encourages innovation and collaboration.

Available at: http://www.iddl.vt.edu/about/mission.php

Note: Used with permission of Virginia Polytechnic Institute and State University Institute for Distance and Distributed Learning.

one day live in a nation where they will not be judged by the color of their skin but by the content of their character" (Stanford University, 1963). This statement, combined with the other elements of his speech, left little doubt to the type of the America Dr. King imagined. His powerful vision still motivates us today.

Value Statement

Values define the institution. They are the basic underlying principles of an organization (McNamara, 1999). Defining these values helps to provide a gauge in which to measure all proposed plans and processes. Perhaps most importantly, it communicates the essentials of the organization that should be both absolute and unwavering. An excellent example of a value statement is demonstrated in the Declaration of Independence. When the authors wrote "We hold these truths to be self-evident, that all men are created equal; that they are endowed by their Creator with inherent and inalienable rights; that among these are life, liberty, and the pursuit of happiness" (The Declaration of Independence, 1776), they provided a statement of values that are still recognized 225 years later.

When examining values in education, there are core values that are shared across academe, and values that are unique to each institution. Thus, the establishment of a value statement often touches on characteristics that are both shared and unique. This provides a comparison that may contrast how an institution attempts to define itself. McNamara (1999) suggests establishing a small number of values, no more than four to six. These values should not be limited specifically to the institution alone; by adapting McNamara's example to online education, the value statement should consider students, administration, faculty, and the community.

Mission Statement

The mission statement is similar to the vision statement; however, it applies to the present. A mission statement should be a call to action. Mintzberg and colleagues (1995) define a mission statement as describing the institution's operations and activities. Bart (1998) provides a more active definition, stating that "a good mission statement captures an organization's unique and enduring reason for being, and energizes stakeholders to pursue common goals. It also enables a focused allocation of organizational resources because it compels a firm [or organization] to

**Table 2.2.   Virginia Polytechnic Institute and
State University Institute for Distance and Distributed Learning
Core Values Statement for Distance Education**

Virginia Tech Institute for Distance and Distributed Learning Core Values:

In support of our efforts, the Institute for Distance and Distributed Learning affirms the following shared core values:

- A shared vision;
- An environment of integrity, trust, and open communication;
- An ideal of excellence, fostered by a belief in quality, teamwork, and service;
- An esprit de corps personified by a positive attitude toward our work;
- A spirit of courage and risk-taking that nurtures creativity and innovation; and
- An appreciation and respect of diverse backgrounds and opinions.

Available at: http://www.iddl.vt.edu/about/mission.php

Note: Used with permission of Virginia Polytechnic Institute and State University Institute for Distance and Distributed Learning.

**Table 2.3.   Virginia Polytechnic Institute and State University Institute
for Distance and Distributed Learning Mission Statement**

The Institute for Distance and Distributed Learning provides leadership, coordination, management, and support to the distance and distributed learning (eLearning) activities of Virginia Tech. As an academic enterprise, the Institute works collaboratively across the university community to:

- Electronically extend Virginia Tech's campus throughout the Commonwealth and beyond;
- Provide an open learning environment where teaching and learning occur anytime and anyplace;
- Share the practical applications of the university's knowledge and expertise to benefit society and support the economic vitality of Virginia;
- Increase Virginia Tech's access to the world and the world's access to Virginia Tech;
- Research eLearning environments and emerging technologies.

Available at: http://www.iddl.vt.edu/about/mission.php

Note: Used with permission of Virginia Polytechnic Institute and State University Institute for Distance and Distributed Learning.

address some tough questions: What is our business? Why do we exist? What are we trying to accomplish?" (p. 56).

A mission statement for online education should be closely aligned with the institutional mission statement. The regional accrediting associations encourage programs to demonstrate support for the institutional mission since programs that are outside of the key mission of the institution are not working toward the common good of the larger organization (Western Cooperative, 2001). Just as the mission statement helps provide direction for the online program, the program's mission statement provides direction for those individuals working under it.

Needs Assessment

The needs assessment is an essential document for strategic planning, as it provides information regarding both the internal and external audiences. An institutional needs assessment reveals key segments throughout the institution where online education has the greatest potential. It should not be limited solely to analysis of the potential external audience alone but should be internally focused as well. Prestera and Moller (2001) urge that a needs assessment "should assess the needs of all stakeholders, including potential and existing students, faculty, administration, and the IT department" (p. 6). All institutions have limited resources—a needs assessment helps to ensure that those limited resources are being allocated in the most effective way.

Despite the seeming ubiquity of the needs analysis in higher education, many institutions appear to be forgoing the needs analysis process for online education. Compora (2003), in his review of six selected colleges and universities in Ohio, found that "none of the institutions surveyed

Table 2.4.   Wichita State University's Recommendation for What a Needs Assessment Should Include

Wichita State University (WSU) has limited resources that can be allocated to support distance education activities. Needs assessments at the community, state, national, and international levels are required to identify program areas where WSU can make a significant impact while remaining economically viable. The Committee feels the following issues and questions are among those that need to be addressed:

- Research should include a thorough search of the education literature to determine the state of the art of distance education to establish a baseline for developing University policy and programs.
- A comprehensive market research study should be performed.
- Administration should determine where WSU possesses a comparative advantage relative to competing universities and for-profit educational businesses.
- It should be determined whether offering not-for-credit courses is central to the University's mission.
- Do complementarities exist between distance education courses developed for academic credit and not-for-credit modules or courses?
- Needs assessment should be an ongoing process.
- Results of needs assessment should be widely distributed across the University to serve as a catalyst for further development of the distance education program.

Available at http://webs.wichita.edu/senate/disted.htm#Needs%20Assessment

Note: Used with permission of Wichita State University.

Table 2.5.   Needs Assessment Examples and Resources

Examples:

- *An Assessment of Training Needs in the Use of Distance Education for Instruction* by Lorraine Sherry and Richard Morse. Available: http://carbon.cudenver.edu/~lsherry/pubs/needs/
- Assessing the need, acceptability, and available resources for adult literacy staff development through distance education in rural Pennsylvania and recommended models to meet the needs by Pennsylvania State University (1993), ERIC Document Reproduction Service No. ED 368 874
- *Distance Education for Interior Design: A Needs Assessment* by Jusri DeVries, MFA, and David B. DiCicco, IDEC, NCARB. http://www.uiah.fi/~jdevries/deid.htm

Resources:

- A Practical Guide to Needs Assessment by Kavita Gupta (Jossey-Bass, 1998)
- *Assessing Needs in Educational and Social Programs* by B. R. Witkin (Jossey-Bass, 1984)
- *Conducting Needs Assessments: A Multidisciplinary Approach* by Fernando I. Sorian (Sage, 1999)
- *From Needs Assessment to Action: Transforming Needs into Solution Strategies* by James W. Altschuld and Belle Ruth (Sage, 2000)
- *Needs Assessment: A Systematic Approach for Successful Distance Education* by Robert G. Stewart and Darcey M. Cuffman (http://www.mtsu.edu/~itconf/proceed98/rstewart.html)
- *Needs Assessment: Goals, Needs, and Priorities* by J. K. Burton and P. F. Merrill. In L. J. Briggs (Ed.), *Instructional design* (pp. 21–45). Englewood Cliffs, NJ: Educational Technology, 1997.
- "Needs Assessment, Needs Analysis, Objectives and Evaluation," by R. Kaufman *Performance and Instruction, 24*, 21, 1985, July/August.
- *Planning and Conducting Needs Assessment: A Practical Guide* by Belle Ruth Witkin and James W. Altschud (Sage, 2001)

indicated that formal internal or external needs assessment were completed" (¶ 3). Institutions that proceed without conducting a needs assessment risk misaligning the institution's limited resources to the needs of its audiences. Compora further suggests that institutions should continue to conduct periodic needs analysis, arguing that it is essential and it must be done in order to continue to meet the needs of the students. Proceeding without a needs assessment places the online program at risk and has potential to waste institutional time, effort, and money.

Like strategic planning, there does not appear to a ubiquitously used format for conducting a needs assessment. Perhaps the best method would be to examine several needs assessments from peer institutions and create an assessment tailored to the specific needs of the institution by selecting the most appropriate elements from numerous assessments.

Goals and Objectives

Goals are somewhat analogous to a construction blueprint. Without a blueprint, it is difficult to understand how the final product should

Table 2.6.   University of Texas TeleCampus Program Goals

Distance Education Goals—General

1. During the next 5 years, the UT TeleCampus will provide a range of programs that are comprehensive, market driven, and based on the needs of Texans as defined most recently by the November 1998 Report of the Texas Strategic Economic Development Planning Commission.
2. These programs should focus on the following Target Market Groups:

   a. Business and Industry Learners
   b. U.T. Component Campus Students
   c. Workforce and Credentials Development
   d. Students in Health Education and the Allied Health Professions
   e. High School Students

3. Programs administered by the UT TeleCampus should focus on Service, Quality, Consistency, and Opportunity.

   • Service: Provide distance education students, associated faculty, and administrators with a superior, service-oriented organization from which to conduct administrative, support, and distance learning activities.
   • Quality: Create a process that encourages collaboration between UT System component institutions and faculty members in the development of high-quality distance education courses and programs.
   • Consistency: Enhance the quantity and quality of educational resource options and services available to current and future UT System students by promulgating consistent standards for component institutions.
   • Opportunity: Support the economic and workforce development needs of Texas, including those identified in the State's Strategic Economic Development Plan.

Distance Education Goals—Specific

1. By Fall 2000, enroll at least 500 students in courses administered by the UT TeleCampus.
2. By Fall 2001, at least one in-service program for public school teachers will be available through the TeleCampus.
3. By Fall 2001, the TeleCampus will be a recognized provider of learning resources and learning assistance to public school students.
4. By Fall 2001, all UT component institutions will have used the TeleCampus to deliver at least one credit or continuing education course.
5. By Fall 2001, the TeleCampus will be able to transfer student registration and grade records transparently between the student's home institution and the institution providing the distance learning course.
6. By Fall 2001, some TeleCampus courses will be taught in multiple sections and may be licensed to institutions other than the originating component institution.
7. By Fall 2001, it will be possible to meet the core curriculum requirements of all components with courses delivered by the TeleCampus.
8. By Fall 2001, all UT components will have an active cadre of faculty and staff who utilize the TeleCampus for delivery of distance education.
9. By Fall 2001, the TeleCampus will be a major provider of in-service education for public school teachers.

Available at: http://www.utsystem.edu/bor/regentalpolicies/DistanceEducation.htm

Note: Used with permission of The University of Texas System.

appear once it is complete. Establishing quantifiable goals and measurements is fundamental to the formation of a healthy online program. Goals provide a description of the work to be done and a quantifiable way to measure when that work has been completed and if it is successful.

Goals should be built upon the foundation of the vision, value, and mission statements. They should also directly address the findings of the needs assessment. Goals that are founded in such a way offer the institution evidence that the program is not only aligned with the mission and needs of the university, but that it is actively pursuing it.

Goals should also be clearly measurable. The measurement of goals ensures that the institution is meeting the standards of quality it has established. In his book, *Make Success Measurable*, Douglas K. Smith (1999) prescribed a proven method. He recommends a concentrated focus on outcomes, not activities, and establishing the measurement criteria during the goal-setting process. For online education, that means defining a specific measurable outcome, such as enrollments, number of classes to be brought online, or course completion rates. There is no magical number of goals that guarantees success; however, generally, the more goals that can be initially established, the better.

Strategies

Strategies should be developed to accomplish the program's goals. Mintzberg (1994) observed a direct relationship between planning and strategy, but suggested they are not identical. According to Mintzberg and colleagues (1995), strategy can be a plan but can also take the form of a pattern, or an institutional practice, which is constant through a period of time. Thus, they propose three forms of strategy:

- Intended strategy—strategy developed from plans.
- Realized strategy—strategy developed from patterns of action, not plans.

Table 2.7.   Wright State University—Distance Education Goals

1. By 2002, 5% of the total courses offered at Wright State University (6,070 courses) should be taught through a distance education format. This percent equals 303 courses.
2. By Fall 2002, 61 courses (1% of all courses) should be offered via compressed video.
3. By Fall 2002, 145 courses (2.4% of all courses) should be Web-enhanced.
4. By Fall 2002, 97 courses (1.6% of all courses) should be offered via full Web delivery.

Available at: http://www.wright.edu/ctl/faculty/dl/proposal/goals.html

Note: Used with permission of Wright State University Distance Learning Unit of the Center for Teaching and Learning.

Table 2.8. Case in Point: Goal Setting—Penn State World Campus

Penn State's World Campus provides an excellent example of establishing goals. The Pennsylvania State University, established in 1855 when the Commonwealth of Pennsylvania chartered the school at the request of the Pennsylvania State Agricultural Society, has grown to be a leader in higher education, with 24 campuses and over 83,000 students systemwide. The Penn State World Campus was established in 1997 to strategically provide online education programs worldwide. The program is led by Dr. Peter Rubba, Senior Director, World Campus. The program is overseen by a steering committee of 23 individuals, all of whom were stakeholders in the World Campus. The World Campus now offers six associate degrees, four undergraduate degrees, seven graduate degrees, and 30 certificate programs to over 5,000 students (representing 11,500 enrollments) on all seven continents, including Antarctica.

President Graham Spanier recognized the potential of online education. In July 1996, he gathered a group of administrators together to discuss Penn State's involvement with online education. Dr. Spanier realized Penn State had three choices: they could choose to not be in online education; get in and grow incrementally; or get into online in a "big way." The group decided that the right choice for Penn State was to wholeheartedly embrace online education.

Dr. Spanier felt strongly that the program should be tied to the mission on the university and should be seen as something not easy to walk away from. The World Campus had to be self-supporting and a generator of new students to the university. Therefore, "the mission of the Penn State World Campus is to provide learners worldwide with access to Penn State academic programs and resources in a sustainable, technology-based learning environment. The World Campus fulfills this mission by:

- offering individual learners and organizational clients convenient and effective access to Penn State credit and noncredit educational programs
- supporting faculty in the creation of learning communities at a distance
- providing mechanisms by which learners can establish a lifelong relationship with the University and its resources.

Shortly after, a discovery group led by Jim Ryan, VP of Outreach, which consisted of campus deans, administrators, and representatives from the faculty senate, assessed the needs of the institution. This discovery group, based on the needs assessment, quickly developed a business plan, and, by March 1997, was ready to begin construction on the World Campus. The output from the discovery group eventually became the first 5-year plan for the World Campus.

Balanced leadership in a policy-based environment allowed Penn State to focus long term and attain balanced and sustainable growth. The World Campus operates as a cost center for the university; therefore, it must recoup its development and operations' cost. The task of creating a funding model that was rewarding to both the academic departments and the university was a challenge. Penn State created a costing model that rewarded academic units by returning 85% of net income back to the academic department. In return for income from the online program, academic departments were required to make long-term commitments to the online program.

A single overriding goal determined the strategy for program scope: to offer key programs where Penn State had a good reputation and dominate that niche. Of the many possible choices, the Turfgrass Management certificate was selected as the initial credit offering because of its unique market characteristics.

The committee also constructed a business plan that emphasized two strategic principles: first, to be self-supporting and create new revenue streams and second, within 5 years, offer 30 programs with 10,000 course enrollments. Creating an environment for 10,000 additional enrollments required thoughtful planning. The World Campus continues to partner with existing campus support structures to integrate the program within the institutional culture and partners with the on-campus instructional design group for faculty support. Throughout this process, instruction and academic responsibility remain with the faculty and existing academic units.

- Emergent Strategy—developed from realized strategy that was not originally intended.

Intended and realized strategies are self-explanatory. Emergent strategies are simply the unintended, unplanned, but successful outcomes that have been incorporated into daily practice. For example, an institution may find that a certain course was originally intended for adult students but has seen enormous growth among the traditionally aged students. When section offerings were increased to meet the demand, and course materials adapted for the younger audience, it created an emergent strategy.

The institution's strategies should be founded upon the previous planning processes, yet should not be so tied to them that emergent strategies are stifled before they have time to develop. Strategic planning alone does not guarantee success, as emergent strategy is also implied. Poley and France (1998) further suggests that "strategies cannot be planned because planning is about analysis and strategy is about synthesis" (¶ 21).

Emergent strategies do yield positive results. In fact, many organizational planning experts suggest that planning (intended strategy) yields a small percentage of the positive results in any organization. Examining a 5-year-old 5-year plan provides evidence to that effect.

What Mintzberg and others recommend is a periodic review that accepts the emergent strategies and to use those unplanned results to work backward through the strategic planning process. Examining emergent strategies may affect or alter the goals, which may bring into question the needs analysis, which may or may not conflict with the mission, values, or vision statements. Any conflict with mission, value, or vision statements should sound an alarm that either the program has grown too far away from its intended purpose or that the mission, value, and vision need to be updated to match the new focus of the institution.

Strategies developed for the online program are as varied as the goals, which may include financial issues, enrollment, faculty incentives, instructional methods, program quality, evaluation, student success, and many others. Ideally, even the decision to employ online education as an instructional method should occur during the strategy formation stage. This stage of the planning process involves more members of the support staff and faculty and less upper-level administrators, if at all. It is at this point that clearly defined documents from the mission, vision, value statements, and the goals begin to guide the actions of institutional personnel as they seek to address the larger institutional priorities.

Of the dozens of strategies institutions can use for online education, three appear to be highly useful and are also the commonly used. These three are not the only strategies used, just the ones that appear to be ubiquitous. These strategies are focusing on a target audience, determining the scope of the online program, and defining a manageable timeline.

Identify the Target Audience

At first glance, it may seem odd for the institution to define a target audience for an online program since the Internet has removed geographical and cultural boundaries. However, defining a target audience allows the institution to draw specific conclusions about demographics such as age, gender, educational needs, and even geographical location. For example, if the institution decides to broaden its focus internationally, administrators must be prepared to deal with increased paperwork to document international student attendance. Concentrating on a smaller target audience lends itself to increased efficiency; after all, marketing to a nationwide audience would require greater resources than marketing to the local community. Additionally, student support services, program policies, recruiting, and exam proctoring will all be affected by the online program's target population.

Defining Program Scope

Institutions should determine program scope by defining which degree plans and courses should be offered online. This allows institutions to better understand what the online program hopes to accomplish, and establish guidelines for policymaking. Starting a program without fully understanding what courses or degrees will be offered is a little like starting a trip without a destination. In fact, Yogi Berra said it best, "If you don't know where you are going, you might not get there" (in Berra & Kaplan, 2001, p. 53).

Unfortunately, not all programs clearly define their scope. Some institutions began by offering prototype courses and treating them as learning experiences for the institution. Starting small and adapting along the way can be an effective way for the institution to learn how it will react to the program and helps to determine the level of support required. However, without a critical mass of students, the campus infrastructure may not be forced to adapt as it would with larger numbers of students. A smattering of courses without a clear direction or goal can lead to wasted efforts by faculty and can result in low student interest.

We believe that an institution is best served by offering at least one complete degree program online. Offering a complete degree program provides several advantages, but perhaps the most valuable is the provision of a marketable product to a specific target audience. In fact, eCollege.com, an eLearning outsource provider, posits that institutions who define their target market have 35.2% greater student enrollments than those institutions that do not (eCollege.com, 1999).

Defining the Timeline

Students need clear communication regarding the scope of the institution's plan for online education. Primarily, students will be interested in how the program applies to them; what value will it offer? Without proper communication, students may make false assumptions such as assuming that all of the courses necessary to complete a degree will be available online. False assumptions may lead to disillusionment and feeling misled.

The institution should determine the order in which degree program(s) and courses will be brought online. There will be competing priorities from various disciplines; choosing between the priorities should be defined by the degree's ability to reach the target audience, meet the objectives of needs assessment, and be effectively offered online. Similarly, individual courses should be scheduled for delivery. Focusing on core courses required for the degree and then moving into supplemental courses is usually an efficient choice.

When constructing a timeline for implementation, the institution must be careful to not be too aggressive in offering more courses than can be properly developed. On the other hand, a schedule that is too conservative hampers the growth of the program and may frustrate students who lack sufficient online courses to complete their degree in a timely manner. Creating a plan that forecasts courses several years in advance also allows the institution to prepare for staffing. A worthy practice is to build in the timeline to the Five-Year-Plan for the entire institution, thus ensuring that the online program is adequately integrated.

Policies and Action Plans

Policies and action plans are the most granular elements of any strategic plan. In fact, they are far more programmatic than strategic, as they relate to day-to-day activities and not visionary plans. Policies and action plans are, however, the conclusion to the planning process, and as such, play an important role in the strategic planning process. They are the final end product and the most detailed of the planning stages. Because policy becomes the framework for institutions to implement their action plans, Chapter 3 addresses the importance of policy and a framework for successful development.

EVALUATION AND ASSESSMENT

Defining quality in online education is difficult at best. The struggle with defining quality is not new, nor is it limited strictly to online education, as academe has struggled with defining success in traditional classrooms for years. When we set out to capture the best practices of successful online

Table 2.9.   Case in Point: Defining the Timeline—
University of Dallas, Graduate School of Management MBA Program

The University of Dallas (UD) is a private, liberal arts, Catholic university founded in 1956 with a current student population of approximately 3,000. UD created its online MBA program in the Fall of 1997, entitling it IMBA--Internet Master of Business Administration. Now students can take the entire MBA core of 11 courses and specialize by taking five courses in any of 10 concentrations such as Health Services Management, IT, and Marketing. More information regarding this program can be found online at http://www.thedallasmba.com.

The program was created by Stan Kroder, Associate Dean of Online Learning, who, after a long career with IBM, joined the University of Dallas to develop and lead the Telecommunication MBA program. Dr. Kroder brought experience in distance learning from IBM. After joining UD he continued to explore various options of distance education that would work for the university. Dr. Kroder created a partnership with a training firm that ran a nationwide satellite network allowing UD to beam its MBA in Health Services to over 1,000 hospitals. He set up another partnership with a large telecommunications company in which UD MBA courses were delivered using the partner's video conferencing network. In 1997, Dr. Kroder first saw the Internet for its potential to deliver online learning and declared, "Now, we can afford our own network!" During the initial semesters, UD partnered with Pace University in New York to offer the inaugural online courses. The online program began with three courses and 30 students. After this initial success, the business school dean "was insistent" the first priority was to get the 11 core courses for the MBA program developed for online delivery. Then, the additional five specialty courses for degree concentrations were added, rounding out an MBA that can be taken totally online or as a blend of online and in-class courses. Today, UD has approximately 800 online students and is still experiencing continued growth. Online students represent over 25% of the UD total MBA enrollment.

UD decided on a Web hosting solution in support of its IMBA. Kroder says, "We have been very satisfied with this approach. Our outsourcing company, eCollege.com, has a very robust network with high availability, a 24/7 help desk, and a very secure platform for course delivery." Kroder continues by saying, "UD professors develop and teach the online courses with assistance from an associate director of online learning. We outsource the running of the system to our partner, eCollege."

education programs, we also struggled with the definition of quality and success. Some programs have accomplished thousands of enrollments, but does that measurement alone constitute success? Other programs have achieved high levels of course completion rates; does that suggest quality? Still other institutions produced graduates who excelled in their disciplines after graduation, so should that apply? The answer lies in looking across all aspects of online education, and holding those aspects to the same accountability standards as traditional programs.

Berge and Schrum (1998) urge that quality standards should remain the same for all students, whether they live away from campus or utilize a different educational delivery modality. In other words, they recommend using the same quality assurance processes as would be followed for an on-campus course. In practice, that's not always easy, as many existing processes and procedures are flawed in their design, evaluating something other than the intended true standard or goal. Because of those flaws, Pond (2002) recognizes the need for changes in quality assessments. He states, "If, however, the point of quality assurance is to truly evaluate quality *and* empower institutions to *improve* the delivery of educational experiences, then we must make fundamental changes in the quality assurance and accreditation paradigms we have relied on for the last 100 years" (¶ 15).

According to Cavanaugh (2002a), top-quality educational content was one of the Web-Based Education Commission's seven critical issues in a report to the U.S. Congress in 2000. We believe the first step in defining quality, and more importantly, increasing quality, is to understand the contributing factors. In fact, both Meyer (2002) and Cavanaugh (2002b), noting the increased interest and need to define quality in online education, challenged all stakeholders to acquire a deeper understanding of the factors contributing to quality. Numerous authors, in their attempt to increase that understanding, have suggested contributing factors. Santovec (2004) found that "successful online programs exhibit two specific characteristics—high-quality course content and faculty that actively engage their students" (p. 1). Moore and Kearsley (2005) suggest, "There are a number of other factors that might be monitored, including: number and quality of applications and enrollments, student achievement, student satisfaction, faculty satisfaction, program or institutional reputation, quality of course materials" (p. 99). Accrediting associations, higher education boards, and councils have proposed numerous additional success factors.

Cavanaugh (2002b) defined a process for assessment of effective distance education that utilizes a three-stage, iterative model she calls the resources–practices–results (RPR) cycle. This model, designed specifically for distance education, consists of the following three stages:

Resources—Procurement and preparation of the resources necessary to meet the distance education goals
Practices—Delivery of instruction using the best practices from education, business, and research.
Results—Analysis of the results of distance education to gauge achievement of the goals.

Under this model, she provided 44 success factors (Table 2.10) "based on decades of research and experience with learners from professions, higher education and K–12 education" (Cavanaugh, 2002b, ¶ 2) summarized from seven authors. Cavanaugh (2002b) matches the established 44

Table 2.10. Distance Education Success Factors

Cathy Cavanaugh (2002a), in *Distance Education Quality: The Resources–Practices–Results Cycle and the Standards*

Resources:
 1. Institutional policy that values distance education
 2. Strategic plan for delivering distance education to students
 3. Stakeholder analysis to determine needs of graduates
 4. Financial commitment that gives the direction regarding program implementation
 5. Team support for distance educators and students
 6. Appropriate technology infrastructure
 7. Program standards to guide course design and delivery
 8. Program review to ensure that all components of the program meet standards and to ensure that the standards contribute to program goals
 9. Effective communication of policies and expectations to students
10. Student services: information, advising, orientation, and security
11. Information privacy
12. Qualified, experienced staff and faculty
13. Community involvement in the program's goals, policies, and outcomes
14. Information provided to faculty about teaching in the distance learning environment
15. Instructor release time for course development
16. Instructor training in distance education pedagogy and technology
17. Course design and delivery assistance
18. Well-designed and appropriate learning materials
19. Student orientation and training
20. Student access to learning resources and instructors
21. Technical support for instructors and students
22. Technology plan to communicate goals to all users

Practices:
23. Focus on content and students
24. Relevant and important skills and knowledge addressed in courses
25. Structured information presented in motivating context
26. Social strategies to promote student comfort, control, challenge
27. Fast feedback from instructors to students
28. Consistent design throughout each course
29. Highly interactive activities for student engagement
30. Authentic communication among students, instructors, and experts
31. Course activities designed to maximize student motivation
32. Activities focused on high-level cognitive skills
33. Development of information literacy
34. Development of applied technical skills

Results:
35. Student independence developed through opportunities for self-assessment
36. Peer review of student work as a professional experience
37. Creation of student portfolios to showcase accomplishments
38. Varied assessments for an accurate view of student abilities
39. Open-ended assignments to increase thinking skills and reduce cheating
40. Secure online testing
41. Ongoing course evaluation by students
42. Evaluation of program by students and faculty
43. Review of program outcomes and components by all stakeholders
44. Program accreditation

Note: Used with permission from the Association for the Advancement of Computing in Education, E-Learn: World Conference on E-Learning in Corporate, Government, Health, and Higher Education 2002(1), Distance Education Quality: The Resources–Practices–Results Cycle and the Standards, pp. 168–173. www.aace.org

success factors against the distance education standards proposed by the various boards, councils, and associations worldwide that have published standards for distance education, to conclude that 31 of the 44 factors were addressed, although no more than 19 by any single entity.

While these 44 factors provide an encompassing list of factors that may be used in evaluation of online education, they do not provide the instruments by which to conduct the evaluations. Creation of an academic evaluation model must include the viewpoints from all participants. Yeung (2002) urges that the institution "will need to conduct study on student's perception on this issue and incorporate the results with the perception of academic staff to form a more complete picture of the whole quality assurance model" (¶ 35). This is important, as Cavanaugh (2002b) observed, "Ultimately, the administration will establish the objectives for the online program and how success and quality will be defined. Moving too quickly through this process will leave the program ill-equipped to address the needs of students, faculty, and the institution" (p. 171). We couldn't agree more.

CHAPTER 3

POLICY AND OPERATIONAL ISSUES

The one who adapts his policy to the times prospers, and likewise that the one whose policy clashes with the demands of the times does not.

—Niccolo Machiavelli

There may be few jobs as diverse as managing the day-to-day operations of an online education program. In a typical day, an online program administrator may work side by side with faculty assisting with the course development process, address technical issues with the IT staff, work on the behalf of a distraught student, develop new institutional policy, assist in developing a marketing strategy, and request budget funds to upgrade the CMS. This chapter addresses the issues that surround the daily operations of an online program. Policy, one of the most important elements to guide the operations of online education, is addressed first, followed by a discussion of duties and organizational structures, and ends with an in-depth dialogue on the financial management and budgeting of the program.

POLICY

Policy has long been used as a tool to direct the efforts of higher education. A review of the literature strongly acknowledges the need for policy to frame and guide online education initiatives. A systematic focus on policy is essential for the online program to become aligned with broader

An Administrator's Guide to Online Education, 31–58

institutional goals and focus individual efforts in a unified direction. While policy should provide a framework for online education, existing policy and/or the lack of appropriate new policy may act as barriers. Thus, modification of existing policy becomes essential in the creation of new policy.

Simonson and Bauck (2003), adapting King, Nugent, Eich, Mlinek, and Russell's (2000) broader definition, defined distance education policy as a "written course of action adopted by an institution to facilitate the development of distance education programs" (p. 417). They later assert, "Policies provide a framework for the operation of distance education" (p. 417). We agree. The creation of policy for online education establishes boundaries and suggests a common direction, thus allowing the institution to focus its efforts in a unified direction. Policy should not be viewed, either by the administration or by the constituency, as simply a list of dos and don'ts; but as Uveges (1971) urged, as "the vehicle institutions use to realize their goals" (as cited in Lape & Hart, 1997). The practice of creating "sound policies should lead to and support sound programs" (King, Nugent, Russell, Eich, & Lacy, 2000, ¶10).

Because distance education is not as prevalent in the minds of faculty and staff as traditional educational practices, policy is needed for guiding decisions and actions that affect distance education. Online education must find relevance as a mainstream institutional methodology if it is to be more than just a niche within academe. Policy helps shift online education activities into the mainstream (Kovel-Jarboe, 1997; Simonson & Bauck, 2003) to find increased importance within the institution. King, Nugent, Russell, and colleagues (2000) also agree that "developing policies in areas where weakness are found is the surest way to help assure that transition from near-randomly offered courses to full-fledged distance education programs" (¶10).

Existing policies must be reviewed, and in many cases, modified, adapted, or completely rewritten (Berge & Schrum, 1998; Birnbaum, 2001; Howard et al., 2004; Johnstone, 2002). Much of the existing policy at most institutions was created to support existing educational paradigms. Howard and colleagues (2004) surmise that "universities will need to transform their structures, rewards, and policies to accommodate the needs of distance education programs" (p. vii). They attest that "historically, universities have designed and built pedagogies, reward systems, organizational structures, procedures, and policies to facilitate face-to-face modes of education. University staff and faculty cling to deep-rooted paradigms, which may have worked well with traditional forms of education, but do not work well for technologically enhanced distance education" (p. vi). Johnstone (2002) noted a similar need for review of existing policy by suggesting that, "For years, students have been held captive by institutional policies and practices that have not been holistically designed" (¶1). The Pennsylvania State University (1996), when implementing their online education program, recognized the need for policy adaptation during the planning process and recommended that any "policies issues as that act as barriers to the use of distance education must be given significant attention and resolved" (p. 19) before proceeding with the online program.

Administrators who seek to modify existing policy should pay particular attention to policy that potentially hinders the growth or acts as a barrier to the success of online education. Birnbaum (2001) urged that particular focus be placed on policy that affects students. Berge (2000) recognized several other policy areas that often act as barriers, such as policies that focus on student issues, institutional partnerships, and faculty participation. Irele (2003, as cited by Gaide, 2004) compared differences in online policy and mainstream policy at four institutions. She found three specific areas of tension created from misaligned policies: faculty issues, student recruitment and retention, and program management and organization.

Modification of existing policies may remove the roadblocks, but new policy is needed to help guide the program to success. With the additional emphasis on technology, new instructional pedagogies, and the increased need for student and faculty support, more policies will be necessary. Koval-Jarboe (1997) found that distance education has stretched the limits of current policy. She emphasizes that "policy and planning must address the unique needs of distance education providers and learners" (p. 23). King, Nugent, Eich, and colleagues (2000) argue that "it is essential to recognize and address the need for new policies where distance learning courses and programs are concerned before institutions can fully and completely address the issues of distance education" (p. 12). In many instances, online education introduces technologies that have not previously been implemented. These new technologies may render existing policies obsolete, thus driving the necessity for the formation of new policy (Katz, 2001).

Creating new policy before implementing an online program sounds good in theory, but isn't always possible, and may not even be practical. Berge and Schrum (1998) posit a synchronized approach to innovation and policy creation is warranted in that "there is a need to conduct instructional planning (including policy and reform) and programmatic implementation simultaneously" (p. 32). Therefore, a strong argument is made that policy may be best developed following a just-in-time approach.

Institutions that follow a just-in-time policy creation approach must work diligently to keep from slipping into a practice of reactive policy change. Berge (1998) observed evidence indicating that in "traditional universities, policies are changed [for distance education] when someone trying to implement a course or program at a distance meets a barrier and through persuasion causes it to be changed or alternatively, develops a work-around to the obstacle" (¶ 7). Gellman-Danley and Fitzer (1998) argue for proactive policy creation, stating that with faculty "even a minor mid-stream policy skirmish can draw the focus away from their most critical concern—teaching and learning" (as cited by Berge, 1998, ¶ 8). Therefore, administrators should be proactive in looking for potential barriers, and work quickly to remove them by adopting or modifying policy before faculty encounter the obstacle.

Policy Analysis

Online education touches many aspects of the institutional structure, requiring numerous policies to be examined. A simple checklist would be ideal but the diversity of organizational structures across institutions limits that approach on a wide scale. Alternatively, several authors have provided broad categories of focus when creating policy. There are two major approaches that have become widely accepted: the seven-tiered Policy Analysis Framework and a simplified three-tiered approach.

The first approach in policy analysis is a seven-tiered model, often described as a policy analysis framework (PAF) (King, Nugent, Russell, et al., 2000) for distance education. The PAF "identifies for decision makers essential, large policy areas as well as particular activities in each area" (King, Nugent, Russell, et al., 2000, ¶5) and has been widely reported and evaluated over recent years (Simonson & Bauck, 2003). Multiple models from Gellman-Danley and Fetzner (1998); Berge (1998); King, Lacy, McMillian, Bartels, and Freddolino (1998); King, Nugent, Eich, and colleagues (2000); and King, Nugent, Russell, and colleagues (2000) were subsequently merged into the most recently published model proposed by Simonson and Bauck (2003). It should be noted that the seventh tier appears to have changed from cultural to philosophical in Simonson's (2002) *Policy and Distance Education*, although no discussion regarding this change was provided in the literature. This is important only because, depending on the institution, the term "cultural" may be more applicable than "philosophical." We believe that these two may be substituted as needed without any major drawbacks. Simonson and Bauck's (2003) version is listed in Table 3.1.

The second approach also follows the PAF approach, but uses a more simplified three-tier model. Several authors have noted that the seven categories listed above appear to perform well for institutional-level pol-

Table 3.1   Policy Analysis Framework

I.   Academic Policies
   A.   Students
      1.   Admission policies
      2.   Grading policies
      3.   Academic records
   B.   Faculty
      1.   Evaluation
      2.   Credentials
   C.   Curriculum
      1.   Accreditation
      2.   Course/program approval
      3.   Course/program evaluation
      4.   Carnegie unit determination

II.   Fiscal, geographic, and governance policies
   A.   Fiscal
      1.   Tuition collection and disbursement
      2.   Special fees
      3.   State funding
      4.   Administrative costs
      5.   Telecommunications costs
   B.   Geographic
      1.   In-district versus out-of-district
      2.   Consortia agreements
   C.   Governance
      1.   Board oversight
      2.   Consortia contracts
      3.   Provider contracts

III.   Faculty Policies
   A.   Compensation
      1.   Design and development incentives
      2.   Overload compensation
   B.   Evaluation
      1.   Course evaluation
      2.   Promotional and contract
      3.   Intellectual freedom
   C.   Support
      1.   Staff development/training
      2.   Course/program support
      3.   Local facilitators

IV.   Legal policies
   A.   Intellectual property
   B.   Copyright
   C.   Liability
      1.   Student
      2.   Faculty
      3.   School

(Table continues)

Table 3.1   Continued

   V. Student policies
       A. Academic
           1. Advising
           2. Resources and laboratories
           3. Training
           4. Testing and assessment
       B. Nonacademic
           1. Equipment and software
           2. Financial aid
           3. Privacy
           4. Access and equity
  VI. Technical policies
       A. System
       B. Contractual agreements
 VII. Philosophical policies
       A. Vision
       B. Mission
       C. Activities

Used with permission from Simonson and Bauck (2003).

Source: Simonson and Bauck (2003, p. 418). Copyright 2003 by Lawrence Erlbaum Associates, Inc. Reprinted with permission.

---

icy but can be overwhelming for smaller organizational units that do not have such broad responsibilities. Therefore, King, Nugent, Russell, and colleagues (2000) propose a less complex three-tiered model that applies to "departments or units engaging in distance education" that "can also be modified to fit within the full range PAF that the larger institution might use" (¶ 8). They suggest that "distance education policy can be studied by looking at large, sweeping areas such as: Students, Faculty, and Management and Organization" and that this abbreviated model offers a more simplified and direct way of addressing policy concerns.

(Reader Note: Rather than provide an extended discussion of policies from the tiered approaches listed previously, deeper discussion and examples of policy are included throughout the book within the chapter and sectional frameworks. Examining other institutions' policies prove to be a productive practice that inspires local policy creation. Other sources, in addition to the example policies provided in this book, may also provide examples of policies that administrators should find helpful.)

Policy creation, in general, has existed within the domain of institutional leadership. When online education is involved, there may not be complete understanding of the many programmatic nuances without participation from individuals who daily manage the program. Therefore, the online program support staff, along with others from selected student

Table 3.2. Resources for Policy Creation

- EDUtools e-Learning Policies: http://www.edutools.info/policy/
- EDUCAUSE/Cornell Institute for Computer Policy and Law: http://www.educause.edu/ EDUCAUSECornellInstituteforComputerPolicyandLawHome/863
- Developing a Distance Education Policy for 21st Century Learning: http://www.acenet. edu/AM/Template.cfm?Section=Search&template=/CM/HTMLDisplay. cfm&ContentID=7819

and faculty support organizations, should be involved in policy development. Moore and Kearsely (1996) agree, stating, along with institutional leadership, "management must also participate in the political process helping policy makers to understand the potential of distance education, obtaining funding, and bringing about the organizational culture change that is needed to accommodate this new form of education" (p. 12). This involvement of managerial personnel in the policy process provides detailed specifics that, in turn, allow the program to reach the desired institutionwide goals more quickly.

ORGANIZATIONAL STRUCTURES FOR ONLINE EDUCATION

Organizational structures for online education are an important element to program success. In fact, Howell, Williams, and Lindsay (2003) believe that success or failure can be directly attributed to its organizational structure. The organizational structure does more than just define the reporting structure; it communicates the program's importance within the institution (Prestera & Moller, 2001).

Organizational structures for online education, not surprisingly, vary dramatically across institutions and are largely determined by institutional culture and existing organizational structures. Verduin and Clark (1991) suggest that structure will be based upon the educational philosophy, social economic, and political restrictions of the institution. While no single dominant practice exists, there are, however, three broad approaches. These might be best described as centralized (a separate, almost autonomous division/college), decentralized (spread across the institution with little if any hierarchal oversight), and a hybrid, resulting in practices borrowed from both approaches. Simonson and colleagues (2003) remind us that Otto Peters's Theory of Industrialization of Teaching provides part of the rationale behind these different approaches. Peters's theory proposes that education can be compared to any industrial practice and thus, educational leaders should seek to apply industrial-styled management approaches to maximize efficiency and minimize cost. Concentration and centralization are key components to Peters's theory.

Bates (2000) and Simonson and colleagues (2003) also note the similarity to industrial organization and propose applying a Fordist framework that is commonly used to describe industrial organizations for describing distance education organizations. In short, a Fordist approach suggests a fully centralized model akin to an assembly line where everything is centrally controlled from a single managerial office. The Fordist approach offers greater economies of scale, making it more attractive to a mass market but lacks little, if any, local control. The second approach, Neo-Fordist, might allow some local control, but still follows a highly centralized model. It is the third approach, described as Post-Fordist, which encourages decentralization but yet still retains integration. This Post-Fordist approach is described by Simonson and colleagues to be when "academic staff would... retain autonomous control over their administered courses, and in so doing, would be able to rapidly adjust course curriculum and delivery to the changing needs of students" (p. 50).

The United Kingdom and others such as the Netherlands, Thailand, Indonesia, and India have adopted Fordist approaches (Bates, 2000), creating mega universities (Daniel, 1998, as cited in Bates, 2000) with hundreds of thousands of students. The United States has, for various reasons, not adopted a Fordist approach at a national level (Bates 2000, Simonson et al., 2003). Bates (2000) notes that in the 1960s, however, Fordist approaches were taken on some U.S. campuses as they rapidly increased in size. The Fordist approach exists today in distance education, where some states have taken a highly centralized approach, combining all distance education efforts into a single organization. Other states have adopted a more post-Fordist approach, allowing multiple institutions to work autonomously.

State legislatures dictate the state-level approaches; however, most institutions maintain control over their distance education organizational structures. Which approach is best at the institutional level? The answer is still being debated internally at many institutions and may only be answered by reexamining the institutional mission.

As for an ideal approach, Bates (2000) believes the hybrid is best. He suggests:

> When it comes to organizational structures, the challenge is to develop a system that encourages teaching units to be innovative and able to respond quickly to changes in subject matter, student needs, and technology. At the same time, redundancy and conflicting standards and policies across the institution must be avoided. Putting too much emphasis on formal organizational structures can be dangerous. Staff willing to work collaboratively will often work around or across organizational boundaries, and perfect

organizational arrangements will not work if petty jealousies and conflicting ambitions get in the way. (p. 181)[1]

One approach that appears to be less successful is best illustrated by what Tony Bates (2000) describes as the "Lone Ranger." Bates defines the "Lone Ranger" as an individual faculty member working independently, without direct support from upper-level administrators (except perhaps for the assistance of a graduate student). He also notes "the Lone Ranger approach is a useful means by which to get faculty members started using technologies, but it is a costly and inefficient method of teaching with new technologies" (p. 2). Can a program under the Lone Ranger model be effective? Yes, but observation reveals that while students gain some benefit from the Lone Ranger, as a whole, students do not receive the amount of support and services needed for success because the Lone Ranger does not have the necessary resources to provide all services. More institutions are realizing that online courses cannot really survive with only a Lone Ranger to lead (Boettcher, 2004a). A dedicated team is needed for success.

How an institution creates the organizational structure is influenced by a variety of factors. Prestera and Moller (2001) suggest that the approach taken at the institutional level will be dependent upon the institution's goals and resources. Existing distance education initiatives and the historical context of similar initiatives within the institution will also have a strong influence on organizational structure. Another sizeable influencing factor will be the skills and qualifications of key personnel and the positions they already hold within the existing organizational structure. Adams and Seagren (2004) note similar findings, and add size and maturity of the distance offerings as factors.

While these factors have significant influence on the organizational structure, they should not override the long-term potential for the program. Administrators should seek an appropriate structure that closely aligns online education with the institutional mission. Berge and Schrum (1998) urged that new programs place distance education administration "where it is most likely to be integrated into the academic mainstream" (p. 7). Pacey and Keough (2003) recognized, "In institutions in which distance education is separated from the mainstream and housed in a separate operating unit, tensions between the campus-based services and distance education services can influence how distance education is conceived and how effectively it can adjust to external environmental factors" (p. 408). Sumler (2004) notes, "Sooner or later, each institution of higher education will reach a crossroads. The institution will have to choose between limiting its activity in online instruction, or adopting management approaches that reduce the cost of online instruction and permit the development of a quality educational product through new strategies such as team course development, consortia sharing of expenses, out-sourcing, etc." (p. 7).

The organizational structure, regardless of the approach, should be kept as flat as possible. Turoff, Discenza, and Howard (2004) warn that "additional organizational layers of intermediaries will doom a program to failure" (p. 15). Flat structures have many advantages, but the most important may be that the organization stays responsive to its stakeholders and is agile and responsive to innovation. Online education is still an evolving medium and changes are still likely to occur.

Another categorization of structure was provided by Mark (as cited in Prestera & Moller, 2001) that better indicates the scope of the structure within the institution. In his model, he defined four types of structures for distance education as: (1) a distance learning program (faculty who develop courses and offer them within their college or department), (2) a distance learning unit (a single entity that operates inside a college or university), (3) a distance learning institution, and (4) a consortium. Of these structures, Sachs (1999) and Prestera and Moller (2001) recommend the unit over the program, citing the numerous efficiencies of a centralized approach. Distance learning institutions, created as separate entities, such as Temple and NYUonline, have not faired as well within the United States. Several have gone under or have been brought back under the control of the traditional institution. Consortia, on the other hand, in various arrangements, continue to thrive and offer institutions numerous possibilities.

CONSORTIA IN ONLINE EDUCATION

Consortia are widely used in distance education. According to the U.S. Department of Education (2003), in the period 2000–2001, 60% of institutions utilizing distance education in the United States participated in some type of consortium. In many cases, the consortium functions as a partner, sharing resources, cooperative purchasing, and perhaps sharing online courses between institutions. In other cases, the consortium may also function like a vendor, providing services for a fee to the institution, which are not part of its core competencies. At times, consortia provide leadership functions within the organization that supply broader goals and work under a separate mission than that of the member institutions.

Institutions will find differing value in consortium participation. For most institutions, the greatest value a consortium can provide will be economic cost savings and superior service (Baus & Ramsbottom, 1999). Consortia such as the Connecticut Distance Learning Consortium (CTDLC), for example, offer services that are of superior quality at a

Table 3.3.   Common Services Provided by Consortia

- Training of Faculty
- Training of Staff
- Access to Leadership Resources
- Articulation Agreements between Members' Institutions
- Cooperative Credit-Sharing Agreements
- Cooperative Purchasing Agreements
- Contract Negotiation
- Course Content and Course Design Services
- Technological Resources such as Courseware Management Systems
- Performance of Need Analyses
- Program or Course Assessments

Table 3.4.   Case in Point:
Consortium—The Connecticut Distance Learning Consortium

The Connecticut Distance Learning Consortium (CTDLC), founded in October 1996, is a state agency and membership organization. It currently supports 46 members, of which 37 are 2-and 4-year institutions of higher education (public and private). The consortium is led by Executive Director Ed Klonoski and began with four pilot courses and the absence of state funding. By 2000, it had grown to 148 courses and 2,000 students and had $500,000 in funding from the State of Connecticut. In Spring 2002, the consortium received $1 million in state funding and has over 5,000 students enrolled with 365 courses and 23 full degree programs. (This program can be found online at http://ctdlc.org)

The CTDLC vision and mission statement states they will "operate as a learning collaborative that enables participating colleges and universities to fulfill their institutional missions while sharing in and contributing to the combined distance learning resources of the consortium" (CTDLC: Mission Statement, 2003). The consortium allows each university to fulfill its institutional mission while also contributing to the combined distance learning consortium. The consortium's formula for success is "to maintain steady but moderate growth, leave technology to the experts, concentrate on pedagogical training, and get those degrees and services online" (Crawford, 2002, p. 38)

Klonoski states the CTDLC is distinct from other consortia in several ways. First, Charter Oak State College acts as a testing resource and a credit bank for aggregating courses from different institutions into degrees. Second, CTDLC tries to keep itself out of the tuition stream--all tuition goes to the institution offering the course. The CTDLC creates revenue for the consortium by offering technology support to its members and provides value to its members by offering services and support. Finally, CTDLC is able to exert control over the courses by offering faculty-development and course-development grants.

CTDLC's most unique feature is its relationship with Charter Oak State College, founded in 1973. This relationship allows students to turn online courses from multiple institutions into a single institutional accredited degree. The college does not actually hold classes and relies on faculty members from other institutions to set the degree requirements for students enrolled in the program. The relationship between CTDLC and Charter Oak has been crucial to the success of both organizations.

Charter Oak State College, led by President Merle Harris, has more than 5,500 alumni and has been regionally accredited by the New England Association of Schools and Colleges Commission on Institutions of Higher Education. Charter Oak State College is located at http://www.cosc.edu.

lower cost than member institutions could provide individually. The CTDLC does this while staying out of the institutions' revenue stream (E. Klonoski, personal communication, April 15, 2003). The economies of scale provide services to member organizations, which is important to the long-term sustainability of any consortia.

Ed Klonoski of the CTDLC recommends having a third party, such as a consortium, perform the needs analysis. He states, "There is too much bias, even unseen bias, when an institution evaluates itself. A third party provides valuable perspective" (personal communication, April 15, 2003).

Some consortia work to provide a mechanism that allows courses to be shared among member institutions. These partnerships rely on creating and maintaining articulation agreements and coordination of courses. Students choose a "home" institution and work to fulfill degree requirements at that institution while selecting courses from a menu of offerings from other member schools.

Consortia, while being helpful to many institutions in many situations, do have their drawbacks. Verduin and Clark (1991) note the most common issues are "philosophical and ideological differences, the potential dominance of one institution over others, problems with sharing costs, and problems with developing learning materials and sharing their use" (p. 176). Perhaps the two largest drawbacks in consortia members that share online courses is competition for students and contrasting course quality.

GUIDANCE COMMITTEE

Many institutions utilize a committee to help oversee the operation of the online education initiative. These committee members, while having diverse roles within the organization, come together for a single purpose: to assist and guide the online education program. This committee's diverse leadership offers two advantages: it infuses a wide range of voices and perspectives into the leadership process and identifies and removes barriers through the creation of policy.

Diversity brings valuable insight in how to best integrate online education into the mainstream institution. Since representatives from key offices within the institution have input to solving the challenges faced by the online program, they are more likely to support the decisions made within the committee. They also serve as a direct communication link between the institution's front-line staff and the Office of Online Education, acting as conduits of information critical to successful operation. Committee-led programs are still, however, largely dependent on an institutional champion. While they are often well managed, committees are

Table 3.5.   Suggestions for Committee Membership

A balance of administrative and academic members provides for a broad cross-representation of the institution. A committee could be represented by some combination of the following:

Academic members
- Academic leadership (provost, associate/assistant provost, dean)
- Department chair(s) from program department(s)
- Online education director
- Instructional designer
- Educational technologist
- Interested faculty who have some degree of online program knowledge/experience
- Librarian (preferably a distance education librarian)

Administrative members
- Administrative leadership (vice president of student services and/or chief financial officer)
- Information technology representative
- Marketing and recruiting representative
- Financial aid, business office, or bursar representative
- Admissions representative

almost always short on the charisma necessary to excite and motivate an organization to change.

Perhaps the greatest advantage to committee leadership is in the creation of policy. Berge and Schrum (1998) specify many policies a committee should address, including fee structures, registration policies, access to educational resources, revenue sharing, and faculty workload. Committees most often have representation from major areas of support as well as involved academic areas. Ideally, all stakeholders would have representation.

DIRECTOR OF ONLINE EDUCATION

Online education programs have a sizeable number of activities to coordinate among numerous departments and organizations, both on campus and off. Prestera and Moller (2001) recommend that someone must coordinate the elements of the program. Most online programs will require at least one full-time employee to oversee online education activities and may often have several more full-time or part-time employees to assist. How these employees are organized and what duties they perform will be largely defined by the distance education structure adopted by the institution. In keeping with the scope of this book, we have chosen to focus on only the common duties found across online education job descriptions.

Often, a single employee bears the responsibility of managing and coordinating all the distance learning activities at the institution. That

Table 3.6.   Case in Point:
Guidance Committee—Dallas Baptist University

Dallas Baptist University (DBU), founded in 1898, is a private Christian, liberal arts university in Dallas, Texas. With a total enrollment of over 4,700 students, this traditional university offers 20 online degree concentrations including a BBA in Management, an MBA in Management or eBusiness, an MA in Organizational Management, and an MEd in Educational Leadership. Information regarding DBU's Online Education program is located at http://www.dbu.edu/online.

Dr. Gary Cook, president of Dallas Baptist University, strongly believed in the traditional campus experience for students, yet he understood the value an online education program offered. In early 1998, he formed a Distance Education Steering Committee and Task Force and commissioned Vice-President of Academics Dr. Gail Linam and Provost Dr. Larry Linamen to co-create this online initiative. The committee includes representation from the library, academic technology, administrative technology, distance education, key vice-presidents, academic advisors, faculty, and deans. This committee proactively developed program policies and procedures and guided the launch of an effective online education program.

Dr. Cook empowered key individuals to prepare the university for the online program initiative. He reallocated necessary budget funds to purchase outside technology support to deliver the first online pilot course in Fall 1998. After this pilot term, Dr. Cook challenged the Distance Education Steering Committee to carry forward with additional courses and degrees offered fully online. DBU initially contracted with eCollege.com for course creation and delivery but later allocated funds to purchase servers and licensing of the Blackboard Course Management System.

Responding to the goals set by Dr. Cook, the committee approved strategic degree programs for online delivery. Dallas Baptist University has experienced growth of more than 1,000 online students, comprising 20% of the institution's total student enrollment. The Distance Education Steering Committee, through policy creation and course and program approval for online delivery, has help DBU maintain high standards of academic quality as the online program maintains a student course completion rate of 92%.

person, often called the Director/Coordinator of Online/Distant/Distributed Education (sometimes having the title Dean, Vice President, or Assistant/Associate Provost), is the person who carries the daily responsibility of overseeing the online education activities. For simplicity, within this book we refer to this person as the Director of Online Education.

Duties of the Director of Online Education

According to Willis (1993), the Director of Online Education assumes a wide range of responsibilities, including consensus building, decision making, and facilitating. This position is largely a managerial and administrative support position and should "maintain an academic focus" (Willis, 1993, p. 34). This individual manages the daily operations of the online program, helps prepare institutional policies and procedures, and acts as both the institutional expert and as a liaison for both faculty and students. It is not uncommon for the program administrator to also train faculty and/or oversee the creation of course content to be used within the online program. Table 3.7 summarizes possible duties and responsibilities that may be included in a job description for the Director of Online Education.

Table 3.7. Common Duties and Responsibilities for the Director of Online Education

Administrative:
1. Coordinates with administration, faculty, and staff.
2. Develop policies and procedures to facilitate distance education initiatives.
3. Insures adherence to pertinent college policies/procedures and regional accreditation best practices.
4. Manages day-to-day operations of program.
5. Identifies and analyzes trends and new developments in distance education.
6. Develops and manages the annual budget and determines program costs.
7. Coordinates proper staffing and training for support of the distance education program.
8. Creates and deploys marketing strategy for distance education program.
9. Prepares grant applications to obtain funding for distance education.
10. Responds or manages the response to data requests from government agencies, private business, the university community, and the general public.
11. Compiles and analyzes of student feedback.
12. Coordinates the preassessment and advisement of students.
13. Develops consortial agreements for distance education delivery partners including developing contacts and negotiating collaborative projects with business, external agencies, and/or educational institutions.
14. Educates and informs constituencies regarding distance education.

Academic:
15. Directs faculty development activities for online education.
16. Collaborates with faculty in analysis, design, and development of course materials.
17. Provides faculty support in design of course materials.
18. Coordinates with academic departments for proper scheduling of courses/degree plans and faculty assignments.
19. Coordinates the development, implementation, and analysis of evaluation and assessment of distance education courses.
20. Oversees the copyright and related issues of using multimedia and instructional materials in distance education courses including licensing and application.
21. Coordinates with necessary departments to ensure student support, including the library, writing center, and testing center, is available for online students.
22. Oversees the compliance of distance education offerings with guidelines for the Americans with Disabilities Act.

Technical:
23. Acts as a liaison between IT staff and faculty to ensure effective operation of distance education infrastructure.
24. Oversees utilization of courseware management system for distance education courses.
25. Assess and evaluate new products used in distance education.
26. Evaluates use of technology for program support.
27. Works closely with IT or outsourced provider for student technical support.

Full-time and part-time employees routinely report directly to the online education director, assisting with the technical and creative aspects of online program management. By contrast, faculty are not as likely to report to the Director of Online Education; however, that varies upon the organizational model utilized by the institution. Those that utilize the distance learning program model (faculty who develop courses and offer them within their college or department) will rarely have faculty report directly; however, those that use the distance learning unit model (a single entity that operates inside a college or university) may. In situations where faculty do report, observation indicates that in most cases these are adjunct faculty that are hired to meet the needs of online enrollment.

Obviously, day-to-day management and coordination must occur. Additionally, policy development and implementation are necessary to program success and the Director of Online Education should be involved in that process throughout the institution, as discussed previously in the chapter. However, there are other duties of the online director that deserve mention. When the duties require that the Director of Online Education oversee faculty development for online course creation and instruction, a delicate balance is needed. The individual should be one part cheerleader, one part facilitator, and one part therapist. This task calls for a person with a strong desire to see the program succeed and a talent for dispelling feelings of ineptitude or inadequacy. Often, faculty who have taught successfully online for several years praise those who initially led them—sometimes kicking and screaming—into online education.

The technical role is two-fold. The director will need knowledge of the courseware management system and other supporting technology influential to the program's effectiveness. The director will also need to communicate regularly with the institutional information technology staff, or outside vendors, to maintain a technoligical infrastructure.

The online education director's most important role may be that of a liaison for the online students and faculty. Online students and faculty will, from time to time, need assistance getting necessary assistance from various departments that support the program. Likewise, the director will represent the online student and/or online faculty in meetings and policy decisions. Acting as a representative for the online program within university organizations and committees often takes large quantities of time and energy as well as diplomacy and skill.

Training and Professional Development

Individuals who oversee online education have a wide range of job responsibilities. Because of the speed in which online education is evolving, online education staff members are dependent on regular training and profession development. Acquiring and maintaining this knowledge base is most often accomplished by attending professional development conferences and seminars and participating in peer networking opportunities.

FINANCIAL MANAGEMENT

Budgeting and financial oversight of online education requires significant involvement. Online programs require considerable financial resources to be successful, yet offer the potential to return significant additional revenue. Accurate planning and forecasting, through the creation of a formal business plan, and the subsequent budgeting process.

Business Plan

A survey of the higher education press offers recent evidence of online education's positive financial impact in the educational market. Shelton and Saltsman (2004) warn, "Higher education institutions must be careful not to become caught up in the same euphoria that swept over the dot-com world [and caution] getting into the market just because everyone else is doing it is a dangerous practice" (p. 21). This "me-too" phenomenon has been well defined. Charles MacKay (1841) wrote about it in his book *Extraordinary Popular Delusions and the Madness of Crowds*. He notes, "Whole communities suddenly fix their minds upon one object, and go mad in its pursuit; that millions of people become simultaneously impressed with one delusion, and run after it, till their attention is caught by some new folly more captivating than the first" (p. 1). While institutions may not be "going mad in its pursuit," we wonder if many institutions are not getting into online education simply because their peers have.

Creating a sustainable online education initiative requires a careful balance between educational quality and financial stability. This equilibrium is sometimes tipped in favor of revenue over academics in the cash-strapped higher education market of today. In a recent interview, former Harvard president Derek Bok recognized this struggle by suggesting, "There are all kinds of ways in which the Internet can improve the quality of instruction. The danger ... to academic values is if you start doing this to try and make a big profit center" (Olson, 2004). Maddux (2003) echoes a similar belief that "the challenge will be to implement distance education in a thoughtful, ethical way, and to do so always with the goal of delivering the best possible education, rather than making the biggest profit"

Table 3.8.   Professional Development Resources for the Online Education Director

Journals and Magazines:
- *American Journal of Distance Education*
- *Australian Journal of Educational Technology*
- *Best Educational E-Practices (BEEP)*
- *Campus Technology Magazine (Syllabus)*
- *Distance Education Report*
- *Distance Learning Magazine*
- *Educational Pathways*
- *EDUCAUSE Quarterly*
- *Electronic Technology in Education*
- *European Journal of Open and Distance Learning*
- *International Review of Research in Open and Distance Learning*
- *International Journal of Instructional Technology and Distance Learning*
- *Journals & Newsletters for Distance Education (C. Darling)*
- *Journal of Distance Education*
- *Journal of Instructional Science and Technology*
- *Journal of Interactive Learning Research*
- *Journal of Interactive Media in Education*
- *Journal of Technology in Education*
- *The National Teaching & Learning Forum*
- *Online Chronicle of Distance Education and Communication*
- *Online Journal of Distance Learning Administration*
- *Open Learning Update*
- *Technological Horizons in Education (T.H.E. Journal)*

Organizations (most offer annual conferences):
- American Society for Training and Development (ASTD)
- American Association for Collegiate Independent Study
- American Association for Higher Education (AAHE)
- American Council on Education (ACE)
- Association for Educational Communications & Technology (AECT)
- Association for the Advancement of Computing in Education (AACE)
- Canadian Association for Distance Education (CADE)
- Council on Law in Higher Education
- The Distance Education Training Council (DETC)
- Electronic Technology in Education
- EDUCAUSE
- Instructional Telecommunication Council (ITC)
- International Council for Educational Media
- International Council for Open and Distance Education
- International Society for Performance and Improvement
- United States Distance Learning Association (USDLA)
- University Continuing Education Association
- Western Cooperative for Educational Telecommunications

Other Conferences:
- Annual Conference of Distance Teaching and Learning
- Distance Learning Administration
- Syllabus

(p. 125). Placing too much emphasis on revenue places the academic quality of the program at risk.

Heerema and Rogers (2001) observed, "If distance education is undertaken with the same goal of effectively generating significant net revenues to subsidize traditional education, then its future will mirror the experience of correspondence education. This is because, as has been seen in the mediation process, as it is presently conceived, forces a trade-off between quantity and quality in higher education" (p. 18). The focus must not be the revenue but the experience of the student, instructor, and the institution.

Conversely, not realizing that academic programs must contribute their fair share to the institution's bottom line can lead to the reverse problem. The business side of online education must be given significant attention. Martz and colleagues (2004) suggest that institutions, even while the majority are nonprofit, should still keep their focus on sound business practices. This can be easily overlooked, as Lane-Maher and Ashar (2001) pointed out that most of the literature and discussion in academe is focused on learning and pedagogy strategies and not on management practices.

For institutions already engaged in online education, as well as for those who are about to start, the creation of a formal business plan is an essential task (Hawkins, 1999). Online education is a complex initiative, touching many institutional processes and divisions. It requires sizeable capital to establish and involves contribution from many individuals. A well-written online education business plan consists of nonfinancial as well as financial elements.

Nonfinancial Elements

A formal business plan is far more than just a spreadsheet. Properly written, the business plan will address the financials, but more importantly, describes the decision-making process (Johnson, 2003) and other operational practices. Brezil (2000) defines a higher education business plan as a document that provides a way to address opportunities in the marketplace, defining the services to be offered, while addressing potential obstacles. The business plan should address, according to Johnson (2003), "funding needs for all phases of course delivery, including design, development, and all dissemination phases" and should also include "questions related to the infrastructure, marketing, recruiting, admissions concerns, counseling processes, assessment, and library and technical support resources" (p. 105). The Southern Regional Education Board's (SREB) Distance Learning Policy Laboratory Finance Subcommittee (2002) recommends a business plan include purpose, market and knowledge of cost implications.

Financial Elements

Obviously, no online program, regardless of successful educational outcomes, can continue if it is not producing sufficient revenue to cover costs (Shelton & Saltsman, 2004). Accurate estimations must be generated. When the financial elements of the business plan are considered, there are three essential elements: costs, revenue, and growth.

Calculation of Costs. Fiscal planning for online programs is not an option, its mandatory (Shelton & Saltsman, 2004) as planning is an essential part of the business plan. Creating an accurate financial goal depends on correctly estimating cost and revenue. As straightforward as this might appear, assessing the true cost of an online program is a matter of debate in academia today since online programs involve significant indirect costs, which are difficult to quantify. For example, the online program may hire an additional online librarian, but that one librarian will rely heavily upon the traditional library organization and infrastructure to be effective. Likewise, institutional student support departments may incur additional responsibilities in the establishment of the online program but without receiving additional staff to distribute the workload.

Compounding the difficulties in estimating cost are calculating fixed and variable costs. Fixed costs, of course, are one-time expenditures, while variable costs increase directly in proportion to the number of students—the more you have the more it costs. Perraton (2000) suggests, "The total costs of a distance education program is a made up of the fixed cost together with the variable cost, that has to be met for each student, multiplied by the total number of students" (p. 120). This leads to the reasonable conclusion that variable costs should be minimized, as increases in students will lead to increases in costs. Bok (as cited in Olson, 2003), notes that from an educational perspective, attempting to minimize the variable costs may not be the best solution. He recognizes that creation of a flashy online course generates a lot of interest and those efforts are fixed costs, but the "highest quality of education capitalizes on the ability of the Internet to provide lots of feedback, interactivity, and discussion among students and faculty, and that tends to be quite expensive" (p. 21).

Cost calculations are not inconsequential. Determining the algorithm to use for cost calculation is a decision to be made individually by each institution during the preparation of the business model. Thankfully, new tools are available that can assist in estimating these costs. Levin and McEwan (2000), in *Cost-Effectiveness Analysis: Methods and Applications*, developed an economic framework that can be applied to educational institutions that helps with policy decisions such as class size. A good in-depth example of calculating cost in distance education is described in "Confronting Cost and Pricing Issues in Distance Education" by Taylor, Parker, and Tebeaux (2001). An additional tool that has also shown to be helpful in estimating the cost of online education is the *Online Cost Calculator* by Brian Morgan at Marshall University (http://webpages. marshall.edu/~morgan16/onlinecosts/). An example is provided in Table 3.9.

Along with cost, income must be addressed in financial planning. For many institutions, estimations of income to cover costs are inadequate, as costs increased much faster than originally expected. McCloskey (2002) echoes similar concerns, noting "in the economics of eLearning cost control is king" (¶ 16). Levine and Sun (2002) suggest these costs are underestimated as "campuses have invested token sums such as a few hundred thousand dollars only to find that the amount is highly inadequate" (p. 8). Carr (2001) reports that administrators are realizing that expanding a program can be more costly than expected. Institutions should therefore include some type of contingency line to the financial plan to account for the probable underestimation of costs.

Table 3.9.   Online Cost Calculator Example

Using Brian Morgan's Online Cost Calculator, consider the following calculation:

- Students currently enrolled in the institution—4,700
- Number of online courses being created—6
- Course developer compensation—$2,500
- Tuition rate—$350/hour
- Technology fee—$40/hour
- Instruction costs—Part of regular teaching load
- Instructional technology support—Yes
- Expected number of students in each online course—22
- Existing server to host courses—Yes
- Expected rate of growth—20%

The following data is returned as an example online program cost:

	Total Costs	Total Revenues
Year 1	$58,541.02	$0.00
Year 2	$105,473.39	$308,880.00
Year 3	$153,733.90	$669,240.00
Year 4	$207,238.06	$1,081,080.00
Year 5	$266,065.18	$1,595,880.00
Year 6	$327,548.58	$2,213,640.00
Year 7	$395,603.78	$2,934,360.00

Table 3.10. Cost Calculation Resources

- *Determining the Costs of Online Courses* by Brian Morgan (http://www.marshall.edu/distance/distancelearning.pdf)
- *Estimating the Conversion Costs of "Online" Courses* (http://academic.algonquincollege.com/staff/aksimr/estimconvcosts.html)
- *Cost Analysis of Online Courses* by John Milam (http://airweb.org/links/reports/costanalysis.html)
- *The Cost and Costing of Networked Learning* by Greville Rumble (http://www.sloan-c.org/publications/jaln/v5n2/v5n2_rumble.asp)
- University of Hawaii Distance Learning Cost Worksheet Components: (http://www.hawaii.edu/ovppp/distlearn/ppp.pdf

---

Calculation of Revenue.   The largest source of income for an online program is derived from student tuition. Since costs and revenue are opposing elements in the financial plan, increasing income is one way to offset the likely increases in costs described in the previous section. Some institutions will have the ability to modify tuition and if the tuition rate is flexible, there will inevitably be a discussion regarding tuition pricing. A case is often made to discount tuition to increase enrollment. The belief is because online students do not require the use of campus buildings, services, or utilities, those savings should be rolled into lower tuition costs that make the online program attractive to potential students. However, others will argue that institutions should increase online tuition because online students require technical support, course management systems, servers, and helpdesk services, all of which are above and beyond what traditional students need.

The question often arises: Does lower cost actually attract students? The question is valid, but there are many other factors involved. Administrators should take into account that higher education is not a commodity purchased at market rates. Each institution will bring an inherent value to its students. Students will factor cost into the equation, but along with many other factors. Marketing experts will be quick to point out that price is only one facet of the marketing mix.

Fees are a second source of revenue. Unlike tuition, fees will be assessed based upon individual services provided. The most common new fees for online programs are technology fees directly related to the increased technology and support costs. If additional fees are to be assessed, a flat fee should be charged for overall support of program operations (Levy & Ramim, 2004).

The institution should evaluate existing fees to determine which are appropriate. When online students pay fees for services they are not receiving, they will feel unjustly charged and complain. Darcy Hardy, Director of the University of Texas System's online education program, describes a classic example. She explains that one of the University of Texas campuses required students to either have private health insurance or to purchase the institution's health insurance package. When a student from Canada enrolled, the institution did not recognize that Canada provided national health care and sent an official notice that he would be required to buy the institutional plan (cited by Carnevale, 2004b, p. A22).

In-State versus Out-of-State Tuition. Distance   education,   especially online education, has created questions regarding residency status and

Table 3.11.   Tuition Policies Examples

University of Montana

Mandatory fees that are not applicable to the distributed learning program will not be assessed. At least one month prior to course or program start-up, the campus shall file notice with the Commissioner's Office of those fees that are applicable to students at remote sites on a course or program basis.

   Available: http://www.montana.edu/wochelp/borpol/bor300/3037.htm

Minnesota State Colleges and Universities: Board Policies

Market-Driven Tuition

Colleges and universities may set and charge market-driven tuition for customized training, continuing education, distance learning, and contract post-secondary enrollment programs.

   Available: http://www.mnscu.edu/board/policy/511.html

Auburn University

Comprehensive Policies: Distance Education Financial Administration

Single Rate/No Fees: All program and course costs, excluding books and materials if desired, shall be calculated as part of the total delivery costs and expressed as a single, per semester hour tuition rate.

   Available: http://web6.duc.auburn.edu/outreach/dl/dlotpolicy.pdf

University of Texas TeleCampus

The individual institutions will be permitted to set the tuition and fees for their own courses in any manner consistent with state law. Specifically, the institutions are already permitted to waive certain mandatory fees for services that are not accessible to students at a distance. In addition, they have the option to waive designated tuition and graduate differential tuition if they deem it appropriate. Courses taught to students who are not residents of Texas and not physically present in Texas may not be submitted for state formula funding (Coordinating Board Rules, Subchapter H). For these courses, campuses may choose to charge traditional out-of-state tuition and fees, or they may choose to charge a flat rate fee for the course (in either case deposited in designated funds accounts).

   Available: http://www.telecampus.utsystem.edu/index.cfm/4,0,85,91,html

Note: Used with permission of University of Montana, Minnesota State Colleges and Universities Board of Trustees, Auburn University and University of Texas TeleCampus.

tuition calculation. Policy is used as a means to clarify tuition costs for online students. Some institutions have continued in-state versus out-of-state pricing for online courses while others have abandoned it. A flat rate of tuition is a common practice regardless on variances of residency status.

Table 3.12.   Tuition Pricing Examples

Colorado State University

The tuition rates for all distance courses are the same for all students regardless of residency status. See individual courses for exact pricing.
  Available: http://www.learn.colostate.edu/distance/tuition.asp

Michigan Community College Virtual Learning Collaborative

In order to facilitate student enrollment in courses offered by provider colleges through the collaborative, a common tuition structure will be established. Tuition rates will be:

In-district, $95/credit
Out-of-district, $135/credit
Out-of-state, $175/credit

Tuition rates will be reviewed periodically by the MCCLV staff and the Michigan Community College Business Officers Association; recommendations for revision will be forwarded to the MCCVLC Governing Committee as appropriate.
  Available: http://www.mccvlc.org/~staff/MOU-3-03.html

University of North Texas
(This policy applies only to out-of-state students.)

Each department may determine the cost for each course in which students residing outside the State are expected to enroll. While the vast majority of these courses will be delivered electronically, this fee also applies to courses in which faculty travel to an out-of-state site to deliver instruction. Departments propose a fee to be charged in lieu of tuition. The proposed fee is reviewed and approved by the college or school and university administration. Departments may make a "profit" on the course.
  Available: http://www.unt.edu/cdl/funding_opps/revised_section/alt_tuition.htm

Northern Arizona University: Tuition and Fees

The NAU Good Neighbor Policy is an Arizona Board of Regents–approved amendment to the requirements for resident status. If you are a non-Arizona resident living in Nevada, Utah, California, or New Mexico (within 75 miles of the Arizona border), you are eligible to pay resident tuition for up to 6 units. If you qualify for the Good Neighbor discount, but wish to take more than 6 units, you will be charged the regular nonresident rate for all units. However, if you enroll in more than 6 units of Web and/or satellite (UniversityHouse) classes only, you will be charged 1.5 times the resident rate for all hours in which you are enrolled.
  Available: http://www.distance.nau.edu/finances/tuition_discounts.aspx

Note: Used with permission of Colorado State University, Michigan Community College Virtual Learning Collaborative, University of North Texas, and Northern Arizona University.

**Table 3.13.   Colorado Commission on Higher Education:
Extended Campus Degree/Non-Degree-Seeking Student Tuition Policy**

3.01.02 Tuition for Non-Credit Courses and
Courses Offering Continuing Education Units (CEU)

Tuition for noncredit and CEU courses shall be set at levels, which ensure that at least full instructional and administrative costs associated with the courses are recovered (Colorado Commission on Higher Education: Extended Campus).

Note: Used with permission of Colorado Commission on Higher Education: Extended Campus.

Degree Seeking versus Non-Degree Seeking.   Many online programs have inherited tuition pricing that allows differences between in degree-seeking and non-degree-seeking students. Online education requires a sizeable level of direct interaction for each student. Policy needs to acknowledge that charges for online courses delivered to non-degree-seeking students may need to be adjusted.

Enrolling auditors or non-degree students into a for-credit course directly increases the instructional cost and support cost. Due to this increase in variable cost, some institutions have policies that increase tuition for non-credit-seeking students enrolling in online courses. Other institutions have adopted a simple "no auditing" allowed policy.

Non-Distant/On-Campus Student Enrollment.   Online course tuition is frequently calculated at rates different than traditional campus tuition rates. In cases where online tuition is lower than on-campus rates, traditional campuses are at risk of losing tuition as students enroll in online classes. In order to eliminate such inequities, many institutions adopted policies that dictate on-campus tuition rates for on-campus students who take online courses.

Similar to the inequalities in tuition costs is the appropriateness of fee calculations for residential students enrolled in online courses. While fully online students do not utilize many of the campus services, on-campus students who take online courses may. Policy should be developed that dictates fee calculations based on residential, commuter, or distance classification.

Estimating Growth.   Growth is an important element in financial planning. The institution should determine the desired rate at which the program should expand. An institution can only support a fixed number of online students; however, a minimum number is necessary for financial validity. Therefore, the institution should establish a necessary minimum and maximum number of enrolled students for each fiscal year.

Table 3.14.   University of Kansas at Lawrence Online Course Fee Policy

Mediated Course Fee. Online courses are subject to a mediated course fee of $30 per credit hour. The distribution of media fees collected from off-campus students is to be as follows: one-third to the University for technology costs, one-third to IDS or Edwards Campus or Continuing Education for instructional support, and one-third to Continuing Education for marketing costs. Media fees collected from students attending the Lawrence Campus will be distributed as follows: half to the University for technology costs and half to IDS for instructional support. Media fees collected from students attending the Edwards Campus will be distributed as follows: half to the University for technology costs and half to Edwards Campus Instructional Development. The Provost may authorize other distributions in cases in which it is warranted (University of Kansas at Lawrence).

Note: Used with permission of University of Kansas at Lawrence.

The issue of maintaining sustainable growth was a problem for many of the early institutions offering online education. Several institutions invested significant resources in the creation of online education programs, developed a substantial infrastructure, but did not have enrollment capable of sustaining the investment. On the other hand, many others had the opposite problem. They invested too little into the infrastructure and student demand quickly outpaced the institution's ability to deliver.

Both of these extremes pose a serious risk to the program and its quality. Programs that do not attract enough students will either operate at a deficit, close, or reduce services and infrastructure. Programs that attract too many students will overwhelm the support structure, which also has implications for quality and long-term sustainability.

When most administrators are asked to project the future number of students in an online program, they simply state: "I have no idea." In fact, many programs originally subscribed to the "if you build it, they will come" model. If a program contained 500 students, great; if it attracted 5,000, even better; if 50,000, "we'd better get busy!" When online education first emerged in the 1990s there was an obvious inability to forecast the popularity of a program. While this broadly impacted campuses, the pioneering efforts of these early adopters have provided valuable experiences. Many institutions were close to their initial predictions. For example, Penn State was able to forecast 5-year growth rates to within 5% of the actual enrollment (G. Miller, personal communication, June 11, 2003). The difference appears to be in the creation of clear and measurable yearly goals that project a sustainable growth pattern over time.

Budgeting

With a good estimate of costs, revenues, and projected growth, institutions can begin the process of budgeting for the online program. Financial reporting structures, like organizational structures, will vary from institution to institution. Of the various reporting structures, is one better than the other? Berge and Schrum (1998) suggest budget-funded programs demonstrate their importance to the institution. This offers the most promise for online education to become part of the institutional mainstream. Ideally, the online program should be budgeted for like any other program, and placed under the same operational reporting requirements, with one key exception. Programs that are in a growth phase must be given ample resources to build the support structure required. Expanding programs, as online education is at most institutions, need resources to grow, develop, and mature.

The Council of Regional Accrediting Commissions, in *Best Practices for Electronically Offered Degree and Certificate Programs*, prepared by the Western Cooperative for Educational Telecommunications (2001), suggests that accrediting associations will want to ensure that the institution's overall business plan and policies for the online program demonstrate an institutional commitment to the online program and its success. Students need to know that the program in which they enroll will be financially sustained throughout the completion of their degree. Accrediting associations will investigate how the online program relates to the overall budget structure, how it is funded, and how the general financial management practices are communicated to the students. Therefore, separate and unique accounting codes must be created and the online program integrated into the institutional budgeting system.

Distribution

Distribution of revenue within the institution or system is an issue that should be clarified by policy. The importance of this policy is heightened when courses are offered outside and between departments where revenue is distributed on a per student basis. Most administrators realize the need to compensate academic units and personnel who developed online

Table 3.15. Southwest Missouri State University Funding Statement

Budgets for Web-based courses must take into consideration both direct and indirect costs, as well as enrollment minimums. This will include expenses for line items such as faculty compensation for course development (where applicable), fringe benefits, marketing, Help Desk costs, equipment maintenance, and course development and technical/administrative resources for faculty and students provided through the Distance Learning and Instructional Technology Center (DLIT) and through the Academic Outreach Department. The course approval process will be contingent on development of a satisfactory budget plan, including a contingency plan in the event that enrollments do not meet budget projections.

Available: http://ce.smsu.edu/dlpolicies/pdf/ppmanual_04.pdf

Note. Used with permission of Southwest Missouri State University.

Table 3.16. Distribution Policy Examples

University of Hawaii

Should projected tuition revenues exceed additional costs (i.e., those costs not covered by the in-kind contributions of originating sites), these revenues are to be distributed 80% to originating campus and 20% to receiving sites.

Michigan Community College Virtual Learning Collaborative

Inasmuch as it is anticipated that both the provider college and the home college will contribute significantly to the success of students enrolled through the collaborative, it is appropriate to share the revenue generated by those enrollments. Tuition revenue will be shared in the following proportions:

Provider college, 70%
Home college, 20%
MCCVLC, 10%

Note: Used with permission of University of Hawaii and Michigan Community College Virtual Learning Collaborative.

course content as well as compensation for instructional costs. Distribution will vary slightly as in-kind contribution, differences in tuition prices, and other variables are figured into the equation.

NOTE

1. *Managing Techolgical Changes*, p. 181, by Tony Bates, copyright © 2000 Jossey-Bass Publishers. This material is used by permission of John Wiley & Sons, Inc.

CHAPTER 4

FACULTY ISSUES

Good teaching is forever and the teacher is immortal.

—Jesse Stuart (1949)

The success of online education is dependent upon the faculty; of course, this is true of any program, traditional or online (Schrum & Benson, 2002). However, because online education is a new paradigm, many faculty are unprepared for the fundamental differences in the roles required for teaching online. The lack of preparation necessitates a higher level of involvement by administrators to ensure success. Bower (2001) further recognizes the importance of institutional support for faculty motivation. Seven issues exist related to faculty that administrators must address: faculty buy-in, policies that address faculty concerns, selection of faculty, faculty compensation, an understanding of faculty workloads, faculty support, and faculty satisfaction.

FACULTY BUY-IN

Faculty buy-in must occur for the online program to be successful and sustainable. The importance of faculty approval and acceptance of the program cannot be overemphasized. Bates (2000) recognized this by writing, "Presidents may dream visions and vice presidents may design plans, and deans and department heads may try to implement them, but without the support of the faculty members, nothing will change" (p. 95). Indeed, fac-

---

An Administrator's Guide to Online Education, 59–81

ulty are needed to move the program forward from the planning phase into the development and implementation phases. Program managers, institutional leadership, and faculty should make faculty buy-in a top priority to.

Faculty are rightfully concerned about the level of instruction and the quality of learning that takes place within their institution. Establishing faculty buy-in is necessary to move the online program into the mainstream campus culture. Yet, Allen and Seaman (2003) note that faculty buy-in is noticeably missing at a sizable number of institutions they surveyed.

Programs that proceed without faculty buy-in are at an increased risk of being marginalized, underfunded, understaffed, or simply shut down. Recently, Allen and Seaman (2003) reported that only 59.6% of institutions surveyed believe their faculty have accepted the authenticity of online education. That leaves numerous programs without faculty buy-in, since the survey also reported in that same time period that 81% of institutions were offering online courses.

Garrison and Anderson (2003) recommend an institution should "delineate a process of basic education aimed at raising awareness of the potential of e-learning if it is to get beyond the early adopters" (p. 109). The movement to accept the program may be slow, as Bates (2000) noted, "In any institution, different faculty members will be in different positions along the change process, which runs the gamut from fear to anger, resistance, grieving for the old, cautious adoption of innovation, and finally total belief in or championing of the change" (pp. 103–104). To achieve faculty buy-in from such a diverse group, the literature suggests providing encouragement and support from administration, faculty involvement in the program development, rewards for faculty participation, and the adoption of policy to facilitate and encourage online education.

Achieving faculty buy-in requires persistence and patience from both administrative and academic leadership. According to Milheim (2001), administrative support should come not from presidents, vice presidents, and the provost alone, but also from deans and department heads because of the roles they play in the development of faculty policy and workload. Administrative leaders, at all levels, should clearly define and articulate the online program's goals and agenda to reveal the institutional vision to the faculty.

Faculty involvement in the development of the online program helps establish faculty buy-in. Prestera and Moller (2001) found "the challenge for distance education staff is instilling the faculty with a sense of ownership while still maintaining some control over the quality and speed of the process" (p. 11). However, administrations often appear to seek efficiency rather than effective teaching (Turoff et al., 2004), which, in turn, discourages faculty participation. Administrators should assure faculty of the institution's commitment to assessment, quality, and maintaining the academic integrity of the program by involving faculty in the quality control process. Faculty participation in a steering or policy-making committee is an excellent strategy that encourages faculty contribution and provides a sense of control within the online program.

Faculty who participate in online education must feel rewarded. Schrum and Benson (2002) suggest faculty need "concomitant rewards" (p. 198). These rewards could be monetary incentives, release time, and/or technology upgrades such as the provision of laptops, software, or the reimbursement of residential Internet costs. The intrinsic rewards, however, can be more important. Research by Rockwell, Shauer, Fritz, and Marx (1999) found that the instructors surveyed were more interested in new techniques of instruction and being recognized for their work and by their peers. Parker (2003) observed similar findings: self-satisfaction, flexible scheduling, and wider audience as intrinsic rewards and stipends, decreased workload, new technology, and release time were the extrinsic motivators. The UT TeleCampus found that providing funding for faculty release time motivated faculty to develop online courses (Saba, 2004).

Finally, faculty need assurance through the creation of policy that the institution has committed itself to online education. Policy provides faculty with evidence the institution is dedicated to enacting the changes necessary to support online education. Martz, Reddy, and Sangermano (2004) agree, asserting that policies communicate reasonable expectations among faculty. Bates (2000) takes a more hard-line approach, suggesting that faculty change only when it is to their advantage. Leadership

Table 4.1. Strategies to Encourage Faculty Buy-In

- Demonstrate high levels of helpdesk and institutional support for course development.
- Demonstrate how online teaching and learning reflects the Socratic method.
- Demonstrate the strengths of online teaching and how it works.
- Emphasize the increased interaction through technology that can result from the online learning community.
- Emphasize the institution's ability to reach students in different geographical/demographic areas.
- Encourage faculty to list inefficiencies of traditional classroom teaching and provide examples of how online teaching can approach these inefficiencies.
- Establish clear policies regarding online education.
- Honestly discuss the negatives of online education and offer solutions or resources.
- List the merits of the delivery such as asynchronous class meetings.
- Openly communicate faculty compensation policy for participation.
- Provide example courses and textbook resource materials for faculty to review.
- Stress the emphasis of online students' personal responsibility for learning.

must reassure faculty of the benefits and possibilities of the online program while simultaneously quelling fears. Adoption of policy provides the clearest evidence of this support.

FACULTY POLICY

Policy not only helps provide faculty buy-in, but it also provides the general framework in which faculty work. Parisot (1997) suggests that the extent faculty use technology as an instructional tool is largely determined by leadership and institutional policy. She further recommends institutions should create policies that support new techniques for teaching. Birnbaum (2001) also urges "that colleges and universities acknowledge the barriers that prevent the implementation and use of distance technologies by faculty, and that these institutions attempt to build a policy that creates and encourages participation" (p. 46). According to Kovel-Jarboe (1997), these policies should also encourage faculty development, which supports the transition of teaching online as distance education requires new roles for faculty.

Policy must be established to provide a framework for online education and to communicate the importance of online education in reaching institutional goals. Policy is needed to address barriers to faculty involvement and help encourage participation (Birnbaum, 2001). Policy is also used as a tool to encourage faculty to try new technologies (Parisot, 1997) and adapt to the changing roles (Kovel-Jarboe, 1997). Perhaps most importantly, policy is needed to demonstrate to faculty the time and effort they invest in online education will be appropriately acknowledged, appreciated, and supported by the administration.

The lack of policy creates issues for faculty (Wolcott, 2003) and increases unrealistic expectations. Online education is still a relatively new instructional methodology and therefore policy should help define faculty responsibilities to help overcome any confusion regarding expectations. Simonson and Bauck (2003) surmise that "faculty need to be recognized for their efforts and expertise in working with distant learners, and until distance education becomes mainstream and expected of all teachers, policies need to be in place that clarify distance teaching responsibilities" (p. 421).

For institutions without formal online education policies, policy creation does not necessarily need to begin from scratch. The American Association of University Professors (AAUP) provides preexisting policy statements that can be either adopted or modified. Additionally, policy statements from peer institutions can also be reviewed and adapted.

Faculty Handbook

A distance education handbook to summarize policy, typical practices, and common procedures is something many institutions find helpful. A handbook provides a tangible list of what is to be expected of faculty and what they can, in turn, expect from the administration in support of their efforts. Willis (1994) proposes, "faculty should be provided with handbooks and other 'take home' materials that clearly and concisely detail a step-by-step process for developing distance delivered education" (p. 284). Examples of distance education handbooks can be found at:

- Cabrillo College: http://www.cabrillo.edu/services/disted/fachandbookintro.htm
- East Tennessee State University: http://de.etsu.edu/Handbook/Handbook.htm
- University of Florida: http://www.doce.ufl.edu/handbook.asp
- Wayne Community College: http://www.waynecc.edu/dist_ed/f-ahandbook.htm

FACULTY SELECTION

The heart of any distance education program is its faculty; for without them, a program could not exist. It has been long acknowledged that "the key to any course's success, whether technology-based or not, is the instructor" (Miller & King, 2003, p. 289). Turoff and colleagues (2004) agree that the instructor's dedication to superior teaching and learning contributes to program success.

Programs must select the most academically qualified faculty available to support the authenticity of the program. Online education programs cannot survive without qualified, dedicated instructors willing to do their very best to engage the student. Husson and Waterman (2002) note, "In the traditional academy, faculty selection is undertaken carefully and rigorously carried out. Evaluation criteria are largely academic, with consideration of other relevant factors dealing with the call to teaching and/or research and publishing. Likewise, the criteria for selection of faculty for distance programmers … should be, first and foremost, academic" (p. 254). Online faculty selection should be principally academic, but not completely. Teaching online shares similarities to teaching in the classroom; however, some consideration must be given to the technical and instructional skills.

In selecting instructors for the online program, it may be that those who are recognized for outstanding teaching in the traditional classroom may not necessarily excel in the online classroom. Online instructors need additional skills to teach in a technical environment where nontraditional instructional methods are often used. Because a faculty member has excelled in one aspect of scholarship does not guarantee they will equally excel in teaching online.

The selection of online faculty should not be based on computer proficiency alone. Potential online instructors should be comfortable in the use of technology; however, some of the best and most effective online instructors identify themselves as "technically challenged" or less-than-capable computer users. Usually, the technology for teaching online can be taught but creating a desire to engage students or increasing the instructor's academic qualifications cannot. Faculty must be motivated to excel in online instruction. The level and quality of the training faculty receive to enrich technical and instructional skills are also directly tied to the success of the faculty members' efforts in teaching online.

Similarly, instructors with high levels of technical proficiency may not necessarily enjoy teaching online. Teaching online requires a certain interpersonal communication style that enables and challenges online students. This teaching style can be described as a coach or personal trainer, one who challenges each student individually and the group as a whole.

Teaching online also requires regularly scheduled time to be devoted to the instruction of the course. This time is often spread across the week and requires more frequent activity than teaching a traditional course might. Faculty who are heavily involved in research, service learning activities, or other time-intensive tasks may not find it feasible to allocate the

Table 4.2. Case in Point: Faculty Selection—Dr. Ron Smiles

Dr. Ron Smiles, a professor of economics at Dallas Baptist University, excels at teaching in both the traditional classroom and online. A two-fingered typist, Dr. Smiles had yet to incorporate any technology into his courses when he was asked to develop an online course. In fact, the college secretary typed many of his exams and course syllabi.

The Dallas Baptist University administration recommended that Dr. Smiles's knowledge and expertise in his discipline be used in the online program. Though past the age of retirement and in spite of his apprehensions and lack of technical proficiency, Dr. Smiles faced the challenge head on.

He was dedicated to the academic integrity of the course and actively worked through the challenges and anxieties of learning a new instructional methodology. After several months of technical training and professional development with the online program director, Dr. Smiles went on to develop three online courses and successfully teaches online each semester—one keystroke at a time.

amount of time required to be truly effective. In such cases, faculty members may be able to serve the institution best in their current roles.

The Adjunct Debate

The dramatic growth in the number of online courses has created a dilemma for many institutions. When the need for courses surpasses the instructors available, the solution is to cap enrollment, pay faculty overload time, or add additional instructors. Most institutions have chosen to hire additional adjunct instructors (Carnevale, 2004a), as the thought of closing classes to interested students is neither popular nor economical. The need to recruit additional instructors is frequently met by hiring adjuncts. Some institutions with large online programs such as the for-profit University of Phoenix have staffed an exceptionally large percentage of their program with only part-time instructors (Olsen, 2002).

Staffing large percentages of online courses with adjunct faculty raises important questions regarding the usage of adjuncts in online education, this has sparked debate at many institutions. The American Federation of Teachers, which represents 1.3 million professors and teachers, is concerned that colleges are taking advantage of adjuncts in online courses and this overuse of adjuncts will cause academic quality to suffer (Carnevale, 2004a). Jamie Horwitz, a spokesman for the American Federation, recently explained in *The Chronicle of Higher Education*, "It's not that online adjuncts don't have the credentials to teach but that instructors ought to be connected with a campus, interacting with other professors and holding office hours" (Carnevale, 2004a, p. A31).

The use of adjuncts in online instruction is an issue that all institutions must address. Encouragement, modification of policy, and creating incentives are all ways to persuade traditional faculty to participate. Even if institutions are successful in persuading full-time faculty to teach online, the institution must still fill the void left by those faculty who are now participating in online courses. Online program leadership should be proactive in seeking approval and advice from the faculty senate or similar governing body in dealing with the need to hire additional instructors. Failure to do so places the program at risk of criticism and brings up questions of legitimacy, quality, and alignment with the institutional mission.

Finding willing and qualified individuals can be difficult, especially if the institution is not in a metropolitan area with a large pool of applicants to draw upon. The use of "distant" distance education faculty has become common practice. Research by FacultyFinder.com showed approximately 60% of colleges and universities in the United States use distant faculty to teach online courses (Adkins, 2004). Distant faculty may need to be recruited nationally, or even internationally. The most effective method is usually to place employment listings in *The Chronicle of Higher Education*, a periodical frequented by qualified and experienced faculty. Other resources include Higheredjobs.com, EDUCAUSE Job Opportunities, FacultyFinder.com, the institutional website, and alumni newsletters.

Faculty Selection Debate

While selection of faculty for traditional programs is almost universally handled within the academic unit, online faculty, adjunct or otherwise, are sometimes hired outside the normal process. Distance education is managed by many models such as a virtual college, an outreach and cooperative extension unit, or under a college/department of continuing education (Schifter, 2000). These units may hire online faculty directly, outside the academic divisions of the traditional campus. Creating separate academic units outside the traditional institution raises legitimate questions of long-term sustainability of the program. The hiring of faculty outside the academic department becomes a highly important decision and one that should be made together by both administrative and faculty leadership. Hiring faculty directly certainly brings efficiency in staffing courses for quickly growing programs, but will it be an acceptable practice for the long term? Each campus culture is different, and it is too early to tell how this may eventually play out academically, but faculty selection is a topic that must be given serious attention and discussion.

FACULTY COMPENSATION

Faculty must find reward in online participation (Kovel-Jarboe, 1997). Most faculty find the intrinsic rewards of online education outweigh the extrinsic rewards (Betts, 1998; Parker, 2003; Rockwell et al., 1999); however, faculty must function in a culture that respects their time, efforts, and intellectual output. This is demonstrated most visibly in compensation and how much consideration online participation is given in the promotion and tenure process (Rockwell et al., 1999; Willis, 1994). Faculty must feel supported and be enthusiastic about participation if the program is to be successful (Willis, 1994).

Compensation and incentives encourage faculty to participate in online activities and reward those that participate. Schrum and Benson (2002) believe that faculty must be rewarded if they are to be successful in the online environment. Incentive structures and policy need to be examined as online education moves mainstream (Koval-Jarobe, 1997). Moving the program to the mainstream requires administrators to focus on compensation, incentives, and perks, and how consideration for promotion and tenure reflects participation in online education programs.

Courseload and Compensation

Courseload consideration for online instruction is the most common form of compensation (National Education Association, 2000). The National Education Association (NEA, 2000) reported 73% of NEA members who taught online courses were compensated as part of their normal courseload. This does not mean that courseload reduction was the exclusive form of compensation, as other enticements such as additional compensation, perks, or other incentives may also be offered.

At most institutions of higher education in the United States, faculty load is calculated in the number of semester credit hours taught. Courseload reductions or equivalencies are routinely given for research or other scholarly activities as well as work in administrative functions. When a faculty member exceeds the teaching load calculations, overload pay, stipends, or other incentives are usually provided. The issue of load is often raised when an institution requests an instructor to develop and/or teach online education courses. Policy should clearly define the institution's calculation of faculty load for course development and instruction. The American Association of University Professors suggests, "The faculty of the college or university should establish general rules and procedures for the granting of teaching-load credit in the preparation and the delivery of programs and courses utilizing distance-education technologies, for required outside-of-class student contact (office hours), and for the allocation of necessary supporting resources" (¶ 11).

Policies should address teaching load for instruction and the initial creation of the online course. Many institutions attempt fair calculation of teaching loads for online instructors by calculating the online course the same as teaching a traditional class. Calculating load for course development is slightly more complex since it is not always limited to a single semester. Schifter (2000) notes that faculty are compensated more for distance course creation than for instruction. Many institutions have adopted a policy of also offering courseload reductions for online course development, but that may not always be enough.

Of course, how the institution chooses to address these issues will be largely based upon culture, historical context, and institutional priority. They should also outline the expectations of faculty to alter or revise the course once it has been developed. The American Council on Education (2000) raised questions regarding not only the creation of the course but also the revision of the course and the amount of time needed to launch the course. In addition to courseload reductions, workload reductions from out-of-class responsibilities may also need to accurately reflect the additional amount of time involved with course creation and modification.

Royalties may be provided as a form of compensation to course developers. As discussed in the intellectual property section of this chapter, payments should be based upon predetermined arrangements and vary from institution to institution. Institutional policy should directly address all concerns regarding the distribution of royalties by explicitly stating whether royalties will be provided or not.

Incentives and Perks

Incentives and perks are also used to encourage faculty participation. Kovel-Jarboe (1997) noted, "When distance learning is a marginal aspect of campus life, it is tempting to offer incentives (often monetary) to entice faculty to design and deliver distance education offerings" (p. 28). Incentives are most often in the form of cash stipends. Other incentives institutions offer are listed below:

- Higher pay for teaching an online class (than for a traditional class)
- Reduction in other workloads (committee, governance, administrative)
- Provision/reimbursement for residential broadband or dial-up Internet access
- New computer hardware or software
- Ability to hold online office hours from home
- Teaching or graduate assistant
- Travel
- National conference fees
- Discretionary spending account (as adapted from Schifter, 2000)

Schifter (2000) found in a study of 160 institutions: the cost of the residential Internet was provided as incentive the most and the provision of a graduate assistant and faculty release time was provided the least.

Promotion and Tenure

When tenure is awarded to faculty, it is usually done based according to formal institutional policy and predefined criteria. The institution's policies toward tenure and promotion communicate the institution's preference for faculty activities, which, in turn, will affect the level of participation by faculty in institutionally approved activities. Rockwell and colleagues (1999) noted that faculty must comprehend how teaching online affects promotion and tenure. Willis (1994) states, "If the institutional reward structure lacks the flexibility to recognize the role played by distance educators, it should be modified before faculty interest and enthusiasm wanes" (p. 288). Bower (2001) further emphasizes that research institutions in particular place an increased emphasis on research activities and not in the development of distance learning courses for granting tenure.

Consideration of online course development and instruction in the tenure and promotion process is a powerful way to encourage participation; not recognizing this will present a sizable issue. The program's champion of change, the leader who presses for acceptance of the online program within the institution, should press for consideration of online activities to be calculated in tenure and promotion criteria. To be effective, online administrators should strive to make sure faculty are evaluated fairly (Willis, 1993).

FACULTY WORKLOAD

Closely related to faculty courseload is the issue of the daily time required to teach online. Workload is not a discussion of how courses count in faculty load calculations, but the number of hours needed each day to teach online. There is a fair amount of discussion regarding the amount of time it takes to teach online taking place across academia. Many faculty are concerned about workload in online courses and that concern has quickly become one of the largest issues in faculty participation. O'Quinn and Corry (2002) surveyed faculty and division chairs at a community college on 30 factors related to participation in distance education. "The factor which posed the greatest concern to all faculty and division chairs regarding their participation in distance education was the workload that faculty incur as a result of participating in distance education" (O'Quinn & Corry, 2002, ¶ 40).

The common conception is "it takes more time to teach in a virtual classroom than in a regular one" (Young, 2002b, p. A31). Many faculty would quickly agree with this assessment; however, in a recent study published in *The Internet and Higher Education*, Hislop and Ellis (2004) found "instructors worked an average of six more minutes per student in an online course than in a classroom. In a course with 30 students, that's about three more hours per semester" (as cited in Carnevale, 2004d, p. A31). Hislop believes the misconception may "result of the pacing of online instruction" (as cited in Carnevale, 2004d, p. A31), as the preparation time is significant before the course starts but slows down throughout the duration. Another study, conducted by Melody M. Thompson comparing workload in the online environment at the Penn State World Campus, found similar results in that workload "was comparable to or somewhat less than that for face-to-face courses ... [noting that] "a differential 'chunking' of productive time contributed in some cases to a perception of increased workload" (Thompson, 2004, p. 84).

This research and other observations suggest that the type of activities a faculty member might be involved in when teaching an online course are different than traditional classroom activities. Rather than spending time in class prep and lecture, an online instructor's time is spent in the discussion boards and responding to email. A focus group conducted with full-time faculty teaching online for the first time at Abilene Christian University revealed that the majority felt they were spending more time grading and less time in direct instruction (Saltsman, personal communication, August 15, 2004). Drexel professor Gregory W. Hislop agrees, stating:

> The hours spent teaching in a classroom tend to come all at once, he says. A professor spends several hours a week preparing a lecture, delivering it, then talking with students after class. In between, the professor rarely interacts with students, besides the occasional office-hour visit or e-mail message. Work for an online course, meanwhile, tends to be more spread out and constant. The frequent contact with online students can interrupt a professor's research or other projects, making it seem that teaching in cyberspace takes more of the professor's time. (as cited in Carnevale, 2004, p. A31)[1]

Class Size

Teacher–student interaction should be encouraged, as it plays a significant role in student attitudes toward online learning (Tomei, 2004). The learning community approach to online teaching requires increased personal interaction to engage with students and effectively ascertain if they are learning and progressing at a desired rate. Therefore, the time a faculty member spends in interaction per student is higher in an online course than in a traditional setting (Tomei, 2004). The best solution to encourage faculty–student interaction, and to obtain the rewards of lower course attrition and greater student performance, is to keep class sizes small.

According to *The Survey of Distance and Cyberlearning Programs in Higher Education, 2002–2003 Edition*, class sizes range from 2 to 100. As for national statistics on average class size, the literature varies from 12 to 15

(Gibbons & Wentworth, 2001) to 20 to 25 (Primary Research Group, 2003; Sausner, 2003). This could be related to sampling errors, exclusion of other distance modalities, timing of the survey, or it may be related to the inclusion of for-profit institutions into the calculations. Interestingly, some of the for-profit institutions, which constitute a sizable number of online enrollments, have lower student–teacher ratios. The for-profit University of Phoenix caps classes at 13 students and has a typical class size of 11 (Olsen, 2002) and Cappella University, another for-profit institution, has an average class size of 12 students (Sausner, 2003).

The classification of the university and level of the course have more to do with predicting class size than anything. In general, the larger the school, the larger the class size. According to Primary Research Group (2003), "Colleges with more than 8000 enrolled students (in all programs not just distance leaning) had an average distance learning class size of nearly 36 students, while all other colleges in all other size categories (all smaller) hovered around 20 per class" (p. 24). The same survey also concluded that graduate courses often have lower class sizes than undergraduate courses (Primary Research Group, 2003).

As far as the ideal class size, for educational outcomes, the smaller the better. Most experts agree that class size should be limited in order to encourage interaction and facilitate the development of a learning community. Student attitudes are driven by the level of interaction with the instructor (Tomei, 2003) and can affect their satisfaction with the course. Sausner (2003) observed that in the beginning, some institutions thought class size would not need to be limited; however, because the important student–instructor interaction increases, the class sizes should be limited. In fact, Sausner found that 20–25 students per class is the best range, while Tomei (2004) calculated that 12 was the most optimal. The Western Interstate Commission for Higher Education (WICHE) does not address class size in their *Best Practices or Electronically Offered Degree and Certificate Programs* document, but suggests "the importance of appropriate interaction (synchronous or asynchronous) between instructor and students and among students is reflected in the design of the program and its courses, and in the technical facilities and services provided" (2001, p. 7). Dropout rates are significantly higher in programs with higher class sizes as well (Primary Research Group, 2003).

From a financial perspective, the more students that *finish* the class, the better for the institution. Many administrators are focused on enrollment numbers, but from a financial perspective, the course completion rate makes the difference. Lynch (2001) cites an institution with dropout rates as high 50%. Since class size has been linked to attrition (Primary Research Group, 2003), lower class size limits may actually return higher numbers of students completing a course. For example, let's assume that

University X caps courses at 40 but experiences a drop rate of 50%, thus yielding just 20 students per course. Meanwhile, University Y caps courses at 25 but has a drop rate of 10%, thus yielding 22.5 students per course. While these numbers are purely speculative, it illustrates the need to keep an eye on course completion rates. If students who drop an online course end up completely withdrawing from the institution, then these losses are compounded exponentially.

FACULTY SUPPORT

Support for faculty teaching online is not optional (Dooley & Magill, 2002). Training must be provided for all faculty members who are asked to participate in the online program. Many authors, like Willis (1994) and Miller and King (2003), believe that training faculty is imperative to online program success. Lee (2001) states, "There is an indication that faculty motivation, commitment, and satisfaction on distant teaching may be in proportion to instructional support they receive" and goes on further to state that "when higher education institutions furnish instructional support to fit their instructor's needs," motivation and commitment are increased (p. 158). Willis (1994) further asserts, "There can be no denying that the ultimate success or failure of the distance education enterprise is inextricably tied to the enthusiasm and continuing support of the faculty" (p. 288).

Evidence is, however, mounting that the current level of support provided to faculty may not be enough. Dooley and Magill (2002) warn that "steps must be taken to increase faculty training and support" (p. 84). Bates (2000) posits, "Faculty members need much more support and encouragement than has been provided to date for their use of technology for teaching and learning" (p. 3). Pankowski (2004) provides some evidence of this need for increased faculty training in a 2002 survey conducted of mathematics faculty throughout the United States. Of those faculty that responded, 89% said that they received some training, but "about half said that the training they received did not adequately prepare them to teach online" (¶ 1).

At many campuses, the online program administrator is charged with providing, arranging for, and in many cases, conducting faculty development for online instructors. The online education office may provide support resources directly, or may work in conjunction with other institutional or consortial entities. Faculty enrichment can be continued with brown-bag workshops, dissemination of relevant books and articles, professional development opportunities, conferences, and brief refresher courses.

**Table 4.3.   Case in Point:
Faculty Support—Maricopa Community Colleges District**

Maricopa Community Colleges District (MCCD) is nationally recognized for its innovation and acceptance of technology and considered one of the pioneering institutions in online education. MCCD is a district of 10 colleges and various satellite centers, located in the state of Arizona. The district offers a support infrastructure, the Maricopa Center for Learning and Instruction (MCLI) (http://www.mcli.dist.maricopa.edu/index.php), dedicated to supporting faculty in the advancement of teaching and learning. This comprehensive center offers opportunities for professional development of online teaching for both full-time and adjunct faculty.

The MCLI provides a carefully reviewed repository of exchangeable ideas and educational models that were developed by the faculty and staff of Maricopa. MCLI's website also provides support for assessment and evaluation, and examples of teaching and learning on the Web.

Training is not only necessary for the creation and teaching of online courses, but in all aspects in which faculty interact with the online program. Moore (1993) proposed that distance education was not just adding technology to teaching, but more about arranging or rearranging the educational resources available. Where possible, training and development opportunities should be tailored to meet the instructor's specific needs. Faculty benefit from peer support; therefore offer support specifically for course instruction and development while giving consideration to establishing formal mentoring programs for inexperienced faculty.

Support for Teaching Online

For online teaching to be effective, instructor support is required. One of the most important elements of that support is training to help orientate faculty into the online classroom. Many instructors found their first classroom experiences disorienting but they quickly adapted, emulating the teaching style of faculty who had personally inspired them and drawing upon years of experience as a student in traditional courses. Faculty members today, however, have little to no experience in online education from which to draw upon. Without that experience, they find it difficult to adjust to online teaching. The attempt to apply teaching methods and pedagogy that work successfully in the traditional classroom does not work as well online, if at all. To help fill this gap in experiences, institutions should work diligently to provide concrete examples and sample online course materials for faculty to build upon.

Online faculty are extremely dependent upon technology for their effectiveness in the course. Obviously, training should be provided to fac-

Table 4.4.　Activities to Help Eliminate
Faculty Apprehension in Online Teaching

- Brainstorm ways of assimilating the professors' favorite classroom teaching methods into the online format.
- Provide examples of ways the learner could be better engaged online than in the traditional classroom.
- Discuss methods for successfully teaching to various learning styles.
- Demonstrate how online class discussions are improved over traditional classroom discussions.
- Illustrate the required participation in online course discussions.
- Emphasize how online students have the opportunity to formulate more eloquent and persuasive responses, including supporting evidence for arguments.
- Install shortcuts on the online instructor's desktop to facilitate easier access to an email program, course management system, or other websites.

ulty who do not possess a basic level of computer proficiency. Faculty also need training beyond basic core competencies. Carol Wilson (2001) conducted a study of distance learning in Kentucky's Higher Education System and found that faculty wanted to use technology but required more advanced support. Offering intermediate and advanced courses for faculty helps improve their technical capabilities as they advance beyond basic technical competency.

In addition to training, faculty need access to technical resources. At the very least, the online instructor needs a capable computer and Internet access. Providing faculty with residential broadband Internet access or allowing faculty to use a loaner laptop while traveling provides additional support. Larger monitors, computer upgrades, and new software are also appreciated.

Assistance with technical issues is best provided by the institution's technology helpdesk. However, since teaching usually extends beyond the hours a campus helpdesk may be open, many online program directors find themselves on call. Providing pager numbers, cell phone numbers, and/or home telephone numbers offers faculty added assurance that they can obtain help whenever necessary. It is not unheard of for program directors or support staff to visit instructors' homes or offices to ensure their Internet connection is correctly configured or to assist with the first online chat session.

Support for Course Creation

Many institutions rely upon their faculty to develop original content for online courses. In 2002, Primary Research found that only 14% of

Table 4.5.   Online Faculty Support Examples

- Arizona State University—Faculty Support: http://asuonline.asu.edu/facultysupport/index.cfm
- Emporia State University—Online Faculty Guide: http://www.emporia.edu/cetech/online_support/facultysupport_blackboard.html
- San Diego Community College District—SDCCD Online Faculty Support: http://www.sdccdonline.net/faculty/index.htm
- State University of New York SUNY—Teaching, Learning, and Technology @SUNY: http://tlt.suny.edu/
- St. Philips College (Alamo Community College District) Online Adjunct Faculty Support Center: http://www.accd.edu/spc/iic/

institutions surveyed used outside providers for online course content. Given the total number of courses online nationwide, that data suggests online course creation has become a major endeavor.

Institutions can provide support to faculty course creators in different ways such as instructional design support including intellectual property and copyright, technical support and media creation, and allowing faculty to work together as a design team rather than individually.

Instructional Design Assistance

A basic understanding of instructional design is necessary to creating good online course materials. Instructional design concepts, however, are not universally understood by all course developers. In fact, for many course developers, creating an online course may be the first time they receive formal instructional design assistance. To meet this need, many programs offer instructional design support for faculty involved in the development process.

Instructional designers, who collaborate with the instructor, begin with the course objectives. Instructional designers then work with the course developer to separate the course content, based upon the course objectives, into manageable learning "chunks" for the student. This process, called "content chunking," is commonly used for developing learning modules for online delivery.

Some programs have developed institutional course templates for instructors to use for online delivery so the content is easily moved into the CMS. Templates, while they may not offer creativity and personality, they do provide the instructor with an easy method for designing course materials.

Intellectual Property

Institutions that create their own content for online courses must address the issue of intellectual property. Institutions should systemati-

Table 4.6.   Recommended Readings for Course Developers

- *Building Learning Community in Cyberspace*, Palloff and Pratt
- *Designing and Teaching an On-line Course*, Schwiezer
- *e-tivities: The Key to Active Online Learning*, Salmon
- *Facilitating Online Learning*, Collison, Elbaum, Haavind, and Tinker
- *Faculty Guide for Moving Teaching and Learning to the Web*, Boettcher and Conrad
- *Lessons from the Cyberspace Classroom*, Palloff and Pratt
- *Moving to Online: Making the Transition from Traditional Instruction and Communication Strategies*, Brewer and Stout
- *The Online Teaching Guide*, White and Weight
- *Teaching at a Distance: A Handbook for Instructors*, Boaz et al.
- *Teaching Online*, Ko and Rossen
- *You Can Teach Online*, Moore, Winograd, and Lange
- *The Virtual Student*, Palloff and Pratt

cally review their intellectual property policy pertaining to course development. This ensures the institution addresses potential concerns raised with the introduction of the online education program and any content created by its faculty for use within the program.

Ownership of scholarly materials used in online courses is a delicate issue between some faculty and administrators. The American Association of University Professors, the American Federation of Teachers, and the National Education Association state that faculty should retain all ownership of course materials. Institutions, understanding the importance of course content to the online program, often seek to retain ownership of courses of which their online programs are dependent. The debate centers on the "work made for hire" stipulation of the U.S. copyright law (which transfers copyright ownership from the content creator to the employer). The institutional support often given to faculty in the form of instructional designers, graphic artists, stipends or release time further confuses the ownership issues.

The issues regarding intellectual property are not superficial. Institutions and faculty must agree before proceeding with course development. Many institutions have developed intellectual property guidelines that are acceptable and amendable to both the needs of the online program and the content creators. One of the more widely chosen policies grants shared ownership to both the content creator and the institution where it retains ownership for use in the online program and the content creator retains ownership for resale or reuse of that material outside the institution.

Copyright

Compliance with copyright law in distance education is important, but unfortunately, is remarkably complex. There have been two major

Table 4.7. Intellectual Property Resources

- Carol Twigg—*Who Owns Online Courses and Course Materials? Intellectual Property Policies for a New Learning Environment* http://center.rpi.edu/PewSym/mono2.html
- Stephen F. Austin University—Policy example: http://www.oit.sfasu.edu/disted/facsup/policies.html
- Indiana University—Policy example: http://www.research.indiana.edu/respol/intprop.html
- University of Maryland University College—Center for Intellectual Property: http://www.umuc.edu/distance/odell/cip/

amendments to U.S. copyright law within the last 7 years: the Digital Millennium Copyright Act (DMCA) and the Technology, Education and Copyright Harmonization Act (the TEACH Act). For distance educators, these acts have spawned both confusion and uncertainty.

The United States enacted the Digital Millennium Copyright Act (DMCA) in October 1998. The DMCA, aiming to update copyright for the digital age, had unintended consequences for distance education and specifically online education. Kevin Wohler (2004) of Washburn University notes, "The idea of Fair Use was effectively removed from Web-based education because of the DMCA." Dolak (2001) likens it to "educational discrimination," noting "a distance learner takes the *same* class as an on-campus student, pays the *same* fees, gets the *same* amount of course credit, has the *same* assignments with the *same* instructor, and receives the *same* diploma. But due to copyright Law, the distance learner does *not* have the same access to classroom audio/visual enhancements as the on-campus student" (p. 2).

On November 2, 2002, the Technology, Education and Copyright Harmonization Act (the TEACH Act) was signed into U.S. law. The TEACH Act, seeking to reverse portions of the DMCA, addresses how accredited, nonprofit educational institutions throughout the United States may use copyright-protected materials in distance education. Specifically, "it amended copyright law to allow college instructors to use nondramatic works, such as news articles and novels, and portions of dramatic works, such as movies, in online courses without paying fees and without seeking the copyright holder's permission" ("College Media Group," 2003).

While the TEACH Act brings much-needed freedom and clarification to the use of copyrighted materials in online education, it is a particularly complex law with no less than 41 requirements ("Teach Act Update," 2005). As if that were not enough, the law was intentionally written vaguely, which may leave institutions open to possible litigation until such a time as the courts have provided an interpretation ("TEACH Act

Update," 2005). In fact, the Consortium of College and University Media Center warned the U.S. Copyright office of a possible conflict between these two federal laws ("College Media Group," 2003). The consortium fears that the anti-circumvention provision of the DMCA, a clause that "makes it illegal to bypass technologies that block access to copyrighted material" ("College Media Group," 2003, p. A29) is not uniformly addressed in the TEACH Act. Others worry about the TEACH Act's vague wording surrounding the "limited and reasonable portions" clause.

Since the TEACH Act is optional, meaning that institutions can choose whether they will accept the allowances that the law provides by agreeing to its stipulations, institutions must evaluate its use. This complexity and exposure has left many institutions on the fence (Dolak, as cited in "TEACH Act Update," 2005). At least one university, Western Washington University, decided not to use the Teach Act, citing uncertainty in "how to interpret key portions" (Carnevale, 2004c) of the TEACH Act.

The number of institutions who have implemented the TEACH Act is unknown. Those who have should review institutional copyright policy to assure compliance ("TEACH Act Update," 2005). Any copyright policy over 2 years old must be updated "to include digital issues before you can [utilize] the TEACH Act" ("TEACH Act Update," 2005, p. 1). The stipulations for implementing the TEACH Act are numerous and places increased responsibilities among various institutional personnel. Dolak (2003) categorized the requirements of the TEACH Act into three categories: institutional, technological, and instructional. Within each category, there are 42 individual activities, which are listed at http://www.bsu.edu/library/media/pdf/teachactchecklist.pdf.

To take advantage of the benefits of the TEACH Act, institutions must be willing to accept certain conditions.

> Among them are the need to adopt and disseminate copyright policies and information resources; implementation of technological restrictions on access and copying; adherence to limits on the quantity of certain works that may be digitized and included in distance education; and use of copyrighted materials in the context of "mediated instructional activities" akin in some respects to the conduct of a traditional course. (Russell, 2002, ¶ 5)

All institutions, regardless whether or not they accept the TEACH Act, must communicate their institutional copyright policy. A best practice adopted by numerous institutions is to provide a copyright overview and/or checklists for appropriate usage on their websites or in training materials for course developers. Georgia Harper, who specializes in copyright law and is the manager of the Intellectual Property Section of the Office of General Council for the University of Texas System, provides an excellent resource regarding copyright issues for online program administra-

Table 4.8.   TEACH Act Resources

- Ball State University—"What is the TEACH Act?": http://www.bsu.edu/library/collections/copyright/complying/
- Georgia Harper—The TEACH Act Finally Becomes Law" 2002: http://www.utsystem.edu/ogc/intellectualproperty/teachact.htm#checklist
- Kenneth Crews—New Copyright Law for Distance Education: The Meaning and Importance of the TEACH Act—American Library Association, 2002: http://www.ala.org/washoff/teach.html#newc
- Laura Gasaway—"TEACH Act Comparison Chart"—University of North Carolina: http://www.unc.edu/%7Eunclng/TEACH.htm
- Peggy Hoon—"The TEACH Tool Kit, An Online Resource for Understanding Copyright and Distance Education"—North Carolina State University: http://www.lib.ncsu.edu/scc/legislative/teachkit/
- The University of Maryland Copyright Policy Repository: http://www.nethics.umd.edu/copyown/policies/index.html

tors and faculty (http://www.utsystem.edu/ogc/intellectualproperty/). The site provides a comprehensive checklist for institutions to verify accountability under the TEACH Act, provides a *Crash Course in Copyright*, and numerous valuable and helpful resources.

Technological and Media Creation Support

One of the most requested resources from online faculty is for technological assistance and support in media creation. There are three general models for providing staff support to assist faculty in the technological aspects of media creation and course development. The first model is to simply assign a student assistant or media specialist to a faculty member for support in course development. The media assistant typically reports directly to the faculty member and spends most of his or her time working directly under the instructor's direction. The second model is to provide a resource in the form of a media creation center in which an instructor brings a request to the center and the center director assigns it to a media developer. In this model, the developers often report directly to the center supervisor and spend their time working with multiple faculty on multiple courses. In the third model, which is a hybrid, the media center assigns an assistant to a professor to work one-on-one for short-term projects, sometimes just a single learning object or perhaps a series of graphics.

Team-Based Course Creation

When developing online courses, faculty may choose to work in teams as opposed to working individually. Team-based course creation, a process in which multiple instructors work together on content creation, is a practice that helps alleviate support by spreading the course development across multiple individuals with multiple talents. Team-developed courses may also allow for improved course content and more complete materials due to the broader range of expertise and experiences from multiple individuals.

Faculty Mentoring

Mentoring is a strategy that provides additional support for online faculty. The benefits from mentoring are not restricted to new faculty members alone, but the process also solidifies and reinforces the mentors' skills. Mentoring programs for faculty can be established with few capital resources, yet provides considerable returns in training and faculty development. Informal mentoring opportunities can be provided at very little cost even if a formal program has not been established by asking experienced and inexperienced faculty to share experiences by socializing at training events, workshops, and other social events.

Most institutions that utilize a formal faculty mentoring program assign an experienced online faculty member to one or more new online instructors for at least one semester and perhaps as long as a year. Instructors who have successfully taught three or more online courses will usually be able to effectively mentor other instructors. Mentors will be able to answer specific questions in regards to the process of teaching online and classroom management, thereby minimizing need for additional support personnel in the office of online education.

FACULTY SATISFACTION

Faculty satisfaction is important for the long-term vitality of the program. Faculty satisfaction not only affects the level of participation but also influences student outcomes (Hartman, Dziuban, & Moskal, 2000). Faculty satisfaction within the online program is an indicator of the effectiveness of the faculty support system, the appropriateness of policies and rewards, and the overall health of the program. It is used as a benchmark to gauge the contentment of faculty who are vital to the success of the program. Faculty satisfaction is important to the academic effectiveness of the courses as it is a variable that impacts student outcomes (Hartman et al., 2000).

Faculty satisfaction should be part of a comprehensive evaluation process. Because of the importance to faculty satisfaction, routine measure-

Table 4.9.   Online Faculty Mentoring Examples

The online education program at Florida Community College at Jacksonville supports a nationwide pool of adjunct instructors. A faculty mentoring program now facilitates online instructor support. Inexperienced online instructors are assigned to a faculty mentor with online teaching experience. This mentor provides support in online teaching, class facilitation, evaluation, and general online instruction questions, both in policy and procedure. Faculty mentors are compensated with a stipend each semester.

Additional Examples of Online Faculty Mentoring are:

* Southwestern College: http://www.swc.cc.ca.us/4thLevel/index.asp?L3=348
* Florida State University: http://online.fsu.edu/instructor/mentor/index.html

Table 4.10.   Areas an Institutional Assessment Should Address

* Are faculty satisfied with online teaching methods?
* Are faculty satisfied with the frequency and quality of training?
* Did faculty feel adequately prepared to teach online?
* Are faculty satisfied with support services such as the helpdesk?
* Was the available technology effective and appropriate for the course?
* What were the instructors' overall experiences in online education?

ments should be performed. Information derived from institutional evaluation is helpful in modifying and improving training, and faculty support systems, as well as adjusting policy.

NOTE

1. From "Whether Online or in a Classroom, Courses Take About the Same Amount of Time," 2004, March 26, p. A31. Copyright by *Chronicle of Higher Education*. Used with permission.

CHAPTER 5

ONLINE STUDENT SERVICES

It is high time that the ideal of success should be replaced by the ideal of service.

—Alexandre Dumas pere

Student support services "play a direct, critical role in student success, including academic performance, psychological growth and program or certificate completion" (SREB Distance Learning Policy Laboratory, 2002, p. i). Unfortunately, institutions have not been as quick to put student services online as they have online courses. This gap in service has left many distance students feeling isolated, frustrated, and alienated. Revamping student services to meet the needs of the online learner is necessary for long-term improvement in online education. Fortunately, tools are available such as the Campus Service Assessment, which allow institutions to take a proactive approach, identifying gaps in service, and thereby enabling institutions to restructure support in the many campus support offices that are needed to serve the distant online learner. This chapter introduces the Campus Service Assessment and examines the numerous services that can be offered in a deconstructed campus support environment.

THE NEED FOR STUDENT SERVICES

Online students' access to student services is vital (Johnson, 2003). The online student, perhaps more than any other student, is removed from personal interaction with the institution. This student is separated not only by geography, but often, the time period in which they desire to do

An Administrator's Guide to Online Education, 83–105

business. The desire for flexibility drives the need for nontraditional methods of interacting with the institutional support services. Online students choose the online medium because it allows them the flexibility to study at convenient hours or in locations far removed from the campus (Matthews, 2002), yet many students are left with inflexible access to even the most basic of student services.

One of the greatest advantages of online education for students is the "anytime-anywhere" approach to learning. A common misconception made by campus administrators is to assume that online students can utilize the institution's support services during normal business hours. In fact, "very few institutions provide a full array of academic and administrative services that can be accessed at anytime from anyplace" (SREB Distance Learning Policy Laboratory, 2002, p. 1). Online students, however, will be quick to assume that 24/7 access to student services will be available (Seehusen, 2000). This difference in expectations creates a noticeable gap in the expected level of service at many institutions.

Another misconception made by administrators is that only a few of the existing campus services need to be placed online. Johnson (2003) suggests a wide range of student services is important to the program's success and Husson and Waterman (2002) see it as a mark of program excellence. Moore (2003) adds, "Learner support is one of the most critical elements in determining the success of a distance education program" (p. 141). Unfortunately, Compora (2003) finds that, "many institutions do not anticipate the commitment to planning and resources that are needed to make [online programs] a true success" (¶ 25). Clearly, there is work to be done in providing more student services to students at a distance. A step in the right direction is to create a "deconstructed" campus service framework.

THE DECONSTRUCTED CAMPUS

A deconstructed campus, as phrased by Sumler (2004), is welcomed by both traditional and distance students. The SREB Distance Learning Policy Laboratory (2002) cites evidence that "services designed to serve distance learners also better serve students who live on or near the campus" (p. i). This is welcome news for administrators who are seeking to maximize their efforts with a minimum of available resources.

The Western Cooperative for Educational Telecommunication's (WCET) Learning Anytime Anywhere Project (LAAP) *Beyond the Administrative Core: Creating Web-Based Student Services for Online Learners* (2003) observed that "today's campus population looks increasingly like the distant population" (¶ 8). Both groups of students have changing attitudes and expectations in an increasingly online-oriented economy. They can pay their cell phone bills online, why not their tuition? WCET LAAP summarizes students' expectations for service with the following traits: self-service where possible, just-in-time, personalized, with customized and customizable service options that can be delivered interactively and that are both integrated with related services and consistent.

Deconstructing, or restructuring student services, is not easy, nor is it cheap. In fact, it may be the most challenging issue for the institution because of the costs and labor needed in redesigning certain procedures (SREB, 2002). Modification of campus support offices to support online students requires planning, patience, and where significant cost is involved, persuasion. Any administrator seeking to modify a long-standing student service infrastructure will be well served in reviewing the WCET *Guidelines for Creating Student Services Online: Lessons Learned* (http://www.wcet.info/projects/laap/guidelines/lessons.asp).

Fortunately, many student support offices over the past few years have been quite active at integrating technology into their service (Kretovics, 2003). However, Kretovics (2003) argues that much of this integration, while a step in the right direction, was accomplished with little thought into the needs of distance students. The disregard for distance students has left institutions with a patchwork of services that do not necessarily serve the distance student effectively or efficiently. Even campuses already involved in distance education may not be equipped to offer online student support in key areas. For example, the 2001 Campus Computing survey noted that less than 30% of responding colleges could accept credit card payments over the Internet (Green, 2001), yet in the same year, the U.S. Department of Education National Center for Educational Statistics (2003) noted that about 54% were offering distance education courses. Where core student service offices do not serve the online student, separate service frameworks must be developed. This is unfortunate because multiple service frameworks are inefficient and are often confusing and frustrating.

Once the campus is deconstructed and services are placed online, the institution should make students aware of the availability of the services (Cain, Marrara, Pitre, & Armour, 2003). Communication of available services is an important element in effective online program administration. In fact, Cavanaugh (2002b) suggests the quality of a program is dependent upon accurate communication to the students.

THE CAMPUS SERVICE ASSESSMENT

Planning is fundamental to moving a campus toward providing service that meets the needs of all students. Institutions must evaluate the students' needs and devise a realistic plan of action before any long-term changes can be considered. Establishing a baseline of services is one of the most important elements in planning. A campus service assessment is a valuable tool to evaluate the institution's current capacity of service and thereby seeks out areas of improvement along with identifying outdated and inappropriate policies.

Evaluating the readiness of the campus infrastructure for online education is a daunting task, yet it should be done before undertaking any student service modifications. The campus service assessment is a process that quantifies the services needed by online students (among others) and tracks the interaction of students with the institution's support structure. According to Boettcher (2004b), "Implementing any institutional or infrastructure design plan often means a realignment of priorities and changes in processes" (p. 33). Cain and colleagues (2003) further emphasized the importance of performing a needs assessment before support services can be designed. The goal of this assessment is to provide a "punch list" of procedures that need to be modified. Once identified, administrators can systematically assess, with quantifiable information, the severity, and prioritize the urgency of each issue.

The campus service assessment can also be simultaneously used as an instrument to identify outdated policies that need to be amended, updated, or removed completely. Inadequate policy is not new. Traditional students have struggled with piecemeal policies for years, but because of their proximity to the campus, have found ways obtain the services they need (Johnstone, 2002). Johnstone (2002) further emphasizes that online students, in contrast, are rarely able to find the services they need in an environment of incongruent, gaping, or overlapping policy. Since many institutions have created policies especially to deal with online students separately, this created an even greater patchwork of policy. Kretovics (2003) urges administrators to challenge the separate but equal notion of serving distance students. Policy adjustments should be made with the desire to serve all students, regardless of location or access to campus, with a single, unified method.

The campus service assessment consists of two major elements. The first is a Student Service Matrix, which identifies key services and their availability to different types of students, with supporting policy documenting current practices. The second is what Ananthanarayanan (2000) calls an information dissemination and communication flow diagram.

The Student Service Matrix quantifies how key student service areas serve certain categories of students. Each student support department would describe the nature of service offered to each classification of students with added commentary, where needed, to define the level of service provided or policies used to determine the level of service. The Student Service Matrix should examine the needs of all types of students,

**Table 5.1.   Sample Categories of Students to
Include in the Student Service Matrix**

- Residential
- Commuter
- Part-time
- Online
- Other distance modalities (i.e., interactive video, telecourses, etc.)
- Handicapped and special needs students

not just one group of students. Table 5.1 lists common categories of students along with the key service areas.

Ananthanarayanan (2000) proposes an information dissemination and communication flow diagram as the second element of the campus service assessment. The Information Dissemination and Communication Flow diagram is a flow chart detailing the communication and interaction between the student and the institution as the student conducts a certain service transaction (see Figure 5.1). Through situational analysis, this document charts the communication flows for each of the categories of students defined in the Student Service Matrix. Where possible, documents such as formal policies, forms, and operational practices/procedures handbooks from offices should be attached to assist in fully documenting the communication flow.

SUPPORT INFRASTRUCTURE

Almost all institutions will require modification to the campus support infrastructure to fully meet the needs of the online learner. The campus

**Table 5.2.   Common Questions the Information Dissemination and
Communication Flow May Answer**

- What requirements must be satisfied for students to gain admittance to a course?
- How should students communicate (toll free/telephone number, email, fax, etc.) with the school to acquire information/support?
- What procedures should students follow in order to access services, such as the library (identification, login, etc.)?
- How do students communicate with advisors and other faculty members?
- How do students access support services?
- What kinds of barriers might students encounter in successfully completing their program and how will the institution remove these barriers? (Adapted from Ananthanarayanan, 2000)

Admissions Workflow for Distant, Online, and Out-Of-State Students

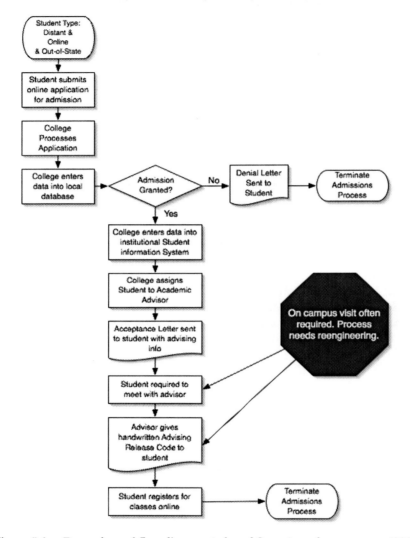

Figure 5.1.   Example workflow diagram (adaped from Ananthanarayanan (2000).

service assessment will have identified most of these inadequacies. Those inadequacies, however, may be numerous, and often come with significant costs and challenges. Nevertheless, action plans should be devised and a plan developed to address the most pressing issues.

Each campus is unique and internal organizational structures vary; however, the student support services provided by campuses are, in general, common to all institutions. *Beyond the Administrative Core: Creating Web-Based Student Services for Online Learners,* a 3-year project funded by the U.S Department of Education's Fund for the Improvement of Postsecondary Education, concluded that the most common services are those that are core services, such as admissions, financial aid, and registration. Table 5.3 provides other services often offered in addition to the common core.

Excellent examples that illustrate exemplary student service are readily available. The remainder of this chapter will highlight these best practices while including accompanying resources, policies, and examples where appropriate. The following outline of services, loosely adapted from *Best Practices for Electronically Offered Degree and Certificate Programs* (Western Cooperative, 2001), highlights the essential services most commonly needed by online learners and provided by successful institutions.

Academic Advising

Academic advising for online students is an important service as they are further removed from typical campus conversations common among faculty and other students. Numerous studies have shown the importance of quality academic advising (Cain & Lockee, 2002). High levels of satisfaction with advising, according to Cain and Lockee (2002), enhances the student learning experience and has even been linked to higher grades. Accreditation associations suggest institutions should provide advising services equally to all students, regardless of status (Western Cooperative, 2001).

Table 5.3. Common Student Services Offered to Online Students

- Academic Advising
- Academic Support (Tutoring)
- Admissions
- Bookstore
- Bursar
- Career Counseling and Job Placement
- Financial Aid
- Library
- Registrar
- Student Community
- Testing

Table 5.4.   Examples of Online Advising Services

- The Community College of Baltimore County's Virtual Advising Centers: http://www.ccbcmd.edu/advisement/online
- University of California Los Angeles: http://www.college.ucla.edu/up/counseling/onlineadvising.htm

When interacting with the student, the more options the student has available, the better. Telephone, live chat, and email are established ways of conducting academic advising for online students. Since many online students wish to conduct business with the institution during nonstandard hours, providing answers to the most commonly asked questions in an Frequently Asked Questions (FAQ) format that can be accessed anytime has proven helpful for students. Furthermore, each question answered by the FAQ reduces the number of responses needed from advisors.

Academic Support (Tutoring)

Online students, like traditional students, require tutoring. Providing academic support to students at a distance can be a challenge. Institutions do not necessarily need to create academic support structures if they do not already exist; however, existing resources should be adapted to serve the online learner. Academic support services for online students may be outsourced or provided at a cost to the student from third-party resources such as SmartThinking (http://www.smarthinking.com) or Link Systems NetTutor (http://www.link-systems.com).

Academic support for online students can be provided through technologies within the CMS, such as virtual chat and discussion boards. Commercial software for academic support also exists and is improving with each subsequent revision. Online collaborative software products that provide Web-based collaboration are also used to facilitate student and tutor communication. The most popular products are:

- Horizon Live (http://www.horizonlive.com)
- Tutornet (http://www.tutornet.com)
- SmartThinking (http://www.smarthinking.com)
- Tutor.com (http://www.tutor.com)

Most approaches are Web-based, seeking to emulate the Web-based learning environment. This is an efficient approach for many situations but support departments shouldn't limit themselves solely to Web-based approaches. Sometimes using fax, email, or telephone are inexpensive and highly effective alternatives. Shared desktop applications such as Timbuktu, PCAnywhere, or the free open source software Virtual Network Computing (VNC) can also provide for collaborative synchronous support environments. These products allow multiple users to interact with a single document in real time, much like working in a group around a single computer.

Admissions

Online applications for admission and the acceptance of admissions documents online have been objectives at most institutions in recent years. Kretovics (2003), citing the 1999 National Survey of Information Technology in Higher Education, indicates that 70% of the surveyed institutions offered online applications and 77% offered access to an online catalog. The provision for accepting online applications is an important

Table 5.5. Writing Center Resources

- Dakota State Online Writing Lab: http://www.departments.dsu.edu/owl/index.htm
- The International Writing Centers Association website (http://writingcenters.org/owcdb/ offers a comprehensive list of online writing centers and resources including links to excellent examples of writing centers online such as Purdue University, University of Texas, and University of Illinois.
- MIT Online Writing Center: http://web.mit.edu/writing/
- Purdue's Online Writing Lab (OWL): http://owl.english.purdue.edu/
- Salt Lake Community College Online Writing Center: http://www.slcc.edu/wc/student
- Trinity College Writing Center: htp://www.trincoll.edu/depts/writcent
- University of Chicago: http://www.uic.edu/depts/engl/writing/
- University of Texas Writing Center: http://uwc-server.fac.utexas.edu/
- University of Wisconsin–Madison Writing Center: http://www.wisc.edu/writing/

Table 5.6. Math Center Resources

- Community College of Denver Online Math Lab: http://www.ccd.edu/asc/math/quickstart.html
- Maricopa Community Colleges Virtual Math Resource Center: VMRC http://mathematics.mc.maricopa.edu/vmrc/
- Ohio University Math Center: http://cscwww.cats.ohiou.edu/aac/tutoring/math/aac_online_math_tutoring.html
- Weber State University Online Math Tutoring: http://weber.edu/assp/mathtutoringlab/online.html
- Whatcom Community College Online Math Center: http:// math.whatcom.ctc.edu/

element for online programs; however, institutions should ensure that all materials related to the admissions process are available online. Online students, more than others, need electronic access to these documents since they are least likely to be able to obtain them in person. Key elements that should be communicated are:

- Estimated costs, tuition, and fees
- Financial aid options
- Availability of student support services (fully online and adapted services)
- Admissions requirements
- Technical requirements
- Description of curriculum design, delivery, and timeframe
- List of courses (available in a fully online format and other distance education modalities). (Western Cooperative, 2001)

Ideally other elements would include links to self-assessment materials, orientation courses, sample course materials, and technology assessment tools.

Bookstore

Students need the ability to purchase textbooks and supplemental course materials. This is most often accomplished by adding electronic commerce capabilities (or by providing mail-order type services) to the institution's bookstore. Other alternatives are to establish a Web presence from an Internet-based bookstore or college bookstore wholesaler such as the Follett Higher Education Group's eFollett.com service. The bookstore website should be linked from several locations within the online program. If certain materials are needed at a specific time in a course, a link to the bookstore should be added.

The office of online education should work with the bookstore to help ensure that accurate communication is flowing between all stakeholders (faculty, students, and administrators). Miscommunication regarding required materials can cause chaos during the beginning of a course. The office of online education should help ensure:

- Timely submission of textbook requests from faculty.
- All instructors, especially adjunct, are aware of the proper procedure for communicating their needs to the bookstore.

- Students are aware of the services that are offered from the bookstore.
- Advanced notice of required materials are sent to students.
- The bookstore accurately understands the need for additional service in helping the online student.

The online students' needs are not limited to textbooks alone. Supplementary materials, such as art supplies, reference materials, lab supplies, lab kits, software, coursepacks, or other pay-per-use licensed academic materials, that are needed in online courses should be made available through the bookstore. Most students also need basic office supplies, notebooks, blue books, or lab journals. While these basic supplies are available elsewhere, institutions that are able to supply these materials to students should find their efforts rewarded with increased purchases.

Bursar

The bursar's office plays a necessary role in supporting online students. Students will receive bills and remit payments throughout their academic careers. Each institution should providing direct access for help to correct billing problems or work with students to devise payment options. The Office of Online Education should be actively involved, establishing communication paths and developing protocols for students to work with the bursar's office. When errors occur, online students need a clearly defined process for working out billing issues without personally visiting the campus.

Obviously, billing is an area where students will demand accuracy. Online education sometimes stretches the limits of the institutional billing systems, as fee structures and tuition for online students vary from those of traditional students. Manually updating online students' bills due to the inflexibility of the institution's financial management software is not an uncommon practice.

When it comes to payment, online students want secure electronic commerce options for paying for tuition, books, supplies, and other necessities. Traditional payment methods should be available but electronic transactions will still be preferred, especially for incidental purchases. Reputable providers should be contracted to handle these transactions if the institution does not already have an electronic payment plan in place.

Career Counseling and Job Placement

Career counseling and job placement services are provided to students to assist with career planning and to help them find gainful employment after graduation. While the entire counseling process does not need to be put online, key elements that allow for initial contact and continued communication should be made available to the online student. In addition, the services that are provided should be clearly described and students should be made aware who is eligible (Western Cooperative, 2000).

Many career centers have worked to place educational materials online. Students may find online modules, or mini-courses, that help in résumé writing, interviewing, and job seeking helpful. In addition to these modules, a core set of basic resources should be made available. Common resources that career centers place online are links to various job search sites, posting of interview opportunities from local or national employers, and documents outlining successful job search skills, resume creation, cover letter creation, or interview techniques.

Financial Aid

Online students are to be given the same financial aid opportunities as traditional students (The Institute for Higher Education Policy, 1998). To achieve that goal, institutions should be proactive in examining financial aid policy and extending services accessible to distant learners. The cost and effort related to provisioning financial aid support for online students mixed with the complexity of federal aid requirements hamper those efforts.

While the details of financial aid administration are outside the daily duties of typical online program administrators, there are key elements that should be understood. The online program should lobby for and work on behalf of the online student to ensure equal access to financial aid. Therefore, a basic understanding of the intricacies of offering financial aid to online students is needed. The following provides a quick overview of the major issues confronting financial aid administration today.

The United States financial aid regulators have labored diligently in recent years to keep pace with the dynamic growth of online education. Many believe that distance education students are being unjustly penalized from receiving federal financial aid. Two rules created the most confusion: the 12-hour rule and the 50-percent rule. The Higher Education Act of 1965 as amended in 1992 enacted what many financial aid administrators call the "12-hour rule" (requires an institution to offer 12 hours of instruction per week to receive federal financial aid). This rule was subsequently relaxed under recent regulatory change yet still raises uncertainty in interpretation for online education. The 50-percent rule, sometimes called the "50–50 rule" (requires an institution to not offer more than 50% of its hours at a distance or have more than 50% of its students at a distance), has also been questioned. At present, institutions can lobby the Department of Education for a waiver to these regulations. Participating institutions that have been granted this waiver are listed at ed.gov/programs/disted/participants.html.

The Higher Education Act, as amended in 2002, made significant progress in addressing "nonstandard" terms (Levine & Sun, 2002). Instruction that provides activities or exams at least one day a week will now satisfy the 30-week academic year requirement. However, this still leaves questions for online education in the interpretation of "one day" and may need to be further interpreted before institutions can take advantage of these changes.

Many higher education administrators expect a full reevaluation of federal financial aid policies in the immediate future (Levine & Sun, 2002). Since many of these guidelines are in a state of eminent change, institutions need to stay alert and ready to alter policy or practices as required. Any changes to policy must be communicated to students as soon as possible and the office of online education should help disseminate that message.

Student Legal Affairs

Unfortunately, harassment, discrimination, stalking, and other unwanted activities can take place in online educational environments, just as in traditional environments. Online students who are being harassed, discriminated against, or in any way being denied their rights must have a process in which to report such actions. The campus police and legal offices should have policies and procedures on responding to and dealing with such inappropriate actions.

Online faculty should be made aware of these policies and be encouraged to quickly request assistance when inappropriate activity is suspected. Institutions may wish to have faculty sign statements that

Table 5.7.   Financial Aid Resources

- Federal Guide to Student Financial Assistance: http://studentaid.ed.gov/students/publications/student_guide/index.html
- Federal Student Website: http://www.students.gov/index.html
- FinAid—The Smart Student Guide to Financial Aid: http://www.finaid.org/
- Free Application for Free Student Aid: http://www.fafsa.ed.gov

Table 5.8.   Financial Aid Good Practice Recommendations from WCET

- Include general information about financial aid. Provide site visitors with basic knowledge of financial aid. Include introductory information to help students understand the different components of the process. Consider including a Frequently Asked Questions format in this section. (University of Wyoming)
- Identify and describe the various types of financial aid available. Inform students of the different financial options available to them, including grants, loans, scholarships, and workstudy. If special financial aid programs are available to assist distance learners, be sure and highlight them. (University of New Mexico)
- Detail the costs of attendance. Provide information on tuition and fees as well as estimates for living expenses and other costs associated with attending your institution. (Northern Arizona University)
- Describe the application process. The steps in the process can often be defined through a checklist. (Eastern Oregon University)
- State all institutional financial aid policies. Define policies and procedures that may affect a student's financial aid and registration decisions. Consider linking to relevant sections of your institution's student handbook or course listing. (Grand Valley State University)
- Link to the online Federal Free Application for Federal Student Aid (FAFSA). Linking directly to this form enables a student to complete an application online. (Metropolitan State College of Denver)
- Provide your Federal School Code for the FAFSA application. Make it easy for students to find your institution's code to list on Federal financial aid applications. (University of Wyoming)
- List deadlines and other important dates. Provide deadlines and other important dates related to financial aid. (Iowa State University)
- Supply other applications and relevant forms. Provide forms for students to download or complete online. Include instructions for each form in a print-friendly format. (Ball State University)
- Link to related sites. Numerous websites already exist that provide useful financial aid information, including http://www.fastweb.com and http://www.collegenet.com. Linking to these sites and others is far easier than developing original material, and it may be more effective. (Azusa Pacific University)

Available at: http://www.wcet.info/resources/publications/guide1003/guide/{268C53DF-C8DB-11D3-9309-005004AD2ACC}_1529.htm

document this training to help protect the institution in the event of possible legal proceedings. Faculty training should offer suggestions that help promote a safe and open environment for academic discussion.

Library

The institution's library is one of the most essential academic resources for the online student. Online students are entitled to the same resources as traditional students, yet they may need additional personal assistance because they are geographically removed from the library. The Association of College and Research Libraries (ACRL), recognizing that right, created the following guideline: "Members of the distance learning community are entitled to library services and resources equivalent to those provided for students and faculty in traditional campus settings" (Guidelines for Distance Learning, 2004).

The challenge for institutions offering online courses is delivering equivalent services without incurring considerable expense. How librarians view their relationship with online students is key. One of the best illustrations of this spirit of service can be found at the Dallas Baptist University's Vance Memorial Library, which adopted the motto, "Equivalent Access—Superior Service" in keeping with standards developed by the ACRL.

Appointment of a distance learning librarian is a common approach to bridge the support gap between distance students and library services. This appointment is also one that is encouraged by the regional accrediting associations. Buchanan (2000) defines this position as a professional that "works closely with departments and instructors to ensure access to materials and services. This person must develop instructional tutorials that can be accessed via the Internet, as well as provide telephone and email assistance to bibliographic instructions" (¶ 11). Institutions may need to appoint at least one distance learning librarian to meet accreditation requirements.

Obviously, the more resources the library has online, the better, but even the most wired library will only be able to offer a small fraction of their materials online. Providing virtual learners access to physical materials requires assistance from the library staff to facilitate this essential service. The most common services libraries provide distance learners for accessing physical materials are:

- Searches to determine appropriateness of materials;
- Retrieving materials, packaging, and mailing;
- Photocopying/scanning of journal materials;
- Photocopying/scanning of micro materials;
- Redirecting interlibrary loan materials; and
- Email, phone, or fax reference services.

In many cases, the library mails these materials to the student via first-class mail. This works well for most students, but not all. Students who are located overseas or who travel frequently are not always able to receive the materials in a timely manner. The practice of delivering scanned materials via email is gaining popularity as a way to reduce institutional cost and increase the speed and convenience of delivery to the student. Networked photocopiers and camera-based scanners greatly assist in the digital delivery of physical materials.

Access to materials alone is not enough; libraries must also provide additional assistance to distant learners to help them in their research. Buchanan (2000) found that students who are "left alone to locate and acquire materials, spend great amounts of time downloading electronic reserve materials, accessing supplementary resources and decipher electronic indexes and databases" (¶ 2). She further recommends for the library to seek out students rather than waiting for students to contact the library for support.

Partnerships between online administrators and librarians are essential. Periodic meetings and regular communication between the online program and the library will be needed to ensure that service to online students is adequate. Each area should alert the other of impending changes in service levels, policy, or approaching problems.

Unfortunately, libraries, like most other academic departments in higher education, have limited resources. The level of service required to serve online students is usually much greater than the level of service provided to traditional students. The differences in levels of service and different classifications of students create ambiguity and confusion among faculty, students, and librarians. Therefore, policy is needed to help remove any ambiguity and provide working definitions of service.

Registrar

Online students rely heavily upon services provided by the registrar's office. Because students need to register for classes, alter schedules, and transfer credit, Johnson (2003) suggests the registrar's office may be the most utilized administrative service by the student. Therefore, ensuring efficient interaction between students and the registrar's office becomes

Table 5.9.   State University of New York College at Oneonta Distance Learner Eligibility for Library Services Example

State University of New York College at Oneonta

All nonresidential students enrolled in distance education SUNY Oneonta courses are eligible for library support services. Distance learner services are not available to students who take one or more courses on the SUNY Oneonta campus. State University of New York College at Oneonta Milne Library http://www.oneonta.edu/library/info/distance/dlearning.html

Note: Used with permission of the State University of New York at Oneonta.

**Table 5.10.   Strategies to Increase
Online Student Awareness of Library Services**

Library services are only helpful to students who are aware of the services offered. Methods used to increase awareness are:

- Send periodic emails to students publicizing the benefits of specific information databases that are relevant to the classes in which they are enrolled.
- Place announcements in the online courseware management system reminding students of services offered.
- Corroborate with faculty to include library resources and assistance in syllabi.
- Create a resource area inside the CRM for instructors to access online databases.

vital. The office of online education should work closely with the registrar's office to ensure that both policy and assistance from the registrar's office are effectively serving the online student.

Registration systems, because of the frequency of use, must be well designed or students will quickly become frustrated. Online registration for online students is almost mandatory; however, other technologies, such as telephone-based registration, are acceptable but less attractive. Administrators must pay special attention to the registration process for the online student and look for ways to improve its usage.

Some institutions allow open enrollment in online courses from all student populations. Other institutions limit registration in online courses specifically for students who are enrolled in distance education programs. When traditional students are allowed to enroll in online courses, the online program director may need to ask for staggered enrollment dates for the online and traditional students to ensure course availability for online students who are limited in their options. For example, at one institution, a policy was implemented that allowed students living over 60 miles from campus to register for online classes before those who lived closer.

Effective communication regarding course offerings and scheduling is imperative. No institution offers all of its courses in an online format and not all online courses are offered each semester. The catalog and class schedule should clearly identify which courses have online sections. Institutions should communicate to all prospective online students a realistic timeline and path for them to follow in order to complete the program (Western Cooperative, 2001). If all the courses needed to complete a degree are not provided entirely online, the exceptions should be clearly noted in the degree plan.

Since many online programs reside outside the institution's traditional academic divisions, it's not uncommon for these programs to have a separate course catalog. A 2000 Primary Research report cited that 42% of online programs surveyed used a separate catalog. Separate course catalogs require special attention and input from the office of online education and the registrar's office. Separate catalogs also create questions of articulation when traditional students take online courses to fulfill requirements in traditional degree plans. Appropriate policy must be developed jointly between the registrar's office and the office of online education to address these issues.

Articulation and course transfer policies for judging and evaluating the courses should not be based on delivery mode. The mode of delivery should not be a consideration but rather the learning objectives and content of the course should be the determining factor in the decision of acceptance (Western Cooperative, 2001). Articulation and transfer policies for traditional and online students must also be consistent throughout the program. Creation of separate policies for online students is a practice that should be avoided (Western Cooperative, 2001).

Student Community

Establishing community and a sense of belonging among online students is an important factor in increasing engagement, involvement, and consequently student success. Students should feel part of the community in which they study, regardless of their proximity to the campus. Creation of community for online students is often overlooked but is an element where accrediting associations are placing increased importance.

Institutions looking for ways to establish community among students have many options. Some ways may be somewhat superficial, like providing methods for students to purchase institutionally branded merchandise, and other may be more involving, such as participation in student government. The overarching goal is to communicate to online students that they are equally important to the success of the institution and that they are equally valued.

Online students need to receive student publications and other materials that help connect them to the institution. Institutional materials and publications such as student newspapers or newsletters help establish community. Whenever possible, these materials should be made available to online students electronically.

Provisions can be made for online students to be included in yearbook and student directories. Washington State University provides a CD-ROM Yearbook for its graduates (LaPadula, 2003). While it seems far-fetched to many, it does send a message that distance students are equally important and just as legitimate as traditional residential students.

Online student governments serve and represent online students at several institutions, the most notable at Washington State University (http://aswsu-ddp.wsu.edu/) and British Open University (http://www2.open.ac.uk/ousa). While this form of student government was created expressly for serving online students, other institutions, choosing not to create separate organizations, have added online student representation to existing student government organizations. While online students may be indifferent to the student government process or outcomes, it still provides them with a way to interact with the university community and offers a channel for their voice to be heard should they choose.

A virtual commons area can also be established to promote socialization among students. Excelsior College provides an example with the Electronic Peer Network (EPN), designed to help students find study partners, chat with other students, and access non-class-related resources. Washington State University provides students with the Speakeasy and Studio Café.

Testing

Many institutions require proctored examinations for online courses. Locating a proctoring facility for online students can be surprisingly time-consuming. In most cases, selection or approval of a testing facility is often left to the faculty member. Ideally, faculty should focus on instruction and not be burdened with the effort of locating, verifying, and communicating with the testing facility for each of their students. Institutions should seek ways to help facilitate the administration of proctored tests. Penn State's World Campus identifies a testing facility for each student at the time of their admittance to the online program. The testing facility and its contact information is stored as part of the student's record and recalled as needed.

Many institutions have begun to participate in testing/proctoring consortia and organizations. The National College Testing Association offers a referral service (http://lorenzo.byu.edu/NCTA/consortium/) to testing centers across the United States and abroad. A regional example can be found in the Texas Computer-Based Testing Collaborative (http://www.tcbtc.org), which provides location and scheduling services for participating Texas colleges and universities. Alternatively, public libraries, public schools, local religious organizations, or local governmental organizations are often agreeable to offer proctoring services at little or no cost to the student.

Serving Students with Disabilities

Students with disabilities have a legal and fundamental right to access higher education, and, subsequently, online courses. Often, students with disabilities are an overlooked market. There are an estimated 54 million persons with disabilities in the United States alone (McNeil, 1997). Students with disabilities are attracted to the increased access offered by online education. Those who may find it physically challenging to attend or participate in traditional courses are often able to participate in online education without the hassles of travel. In fact, Kinash, Crichton, and Kim-Rupnow (2004) found the time- and location-independent format that exemplifies the pedagogy of online education may be best suited for physically challenged students to participate in formal higher education. However, they found that persons with disabilities are "among the least considered in the educational context of online learning" (p. 5).

There is a nationwide movement in the United States to design courses that are accessible by persons with disabilities. This movement, in some part, is mandated by federal laws, which include the Americans with Disabilities Act (ADA) of 1990, Section 504 of the Vocational Rehabilitation Act (1973), and the 1998 Amendment to Section 508 of the Vocational Rehabilitation Act. Title II of the ADA, which applies to public entities, and Title III, which applies to public accommodation, also directly affects higher education institutions. In 1996, the Department of Justice interpreted the Americans with Disabilities Act as requiring institutions to provide "effective communications" (Patrick, 1996, as cited in Edmonds, 2004a, p. 54). The practicality of this ruling implies that websites for online education must be viewable using adaptive technology devices. Exceptions only exist where these provisions would fundamentally change the instruction or create undue burden on the institution. In addition to ADA, Section 504 of the Vocational Rehabilitation Act was amended in 1998 to ensure that any information technology a federal agency acquires must be accessible as long as it does not present an undue burden (Edmonds, 2004b).

Section 508 of the 1998 Amendment to the Vocational Rehabilitation Act (1973) has the most implication for online education. Under Section 508, "federal agencies must give employees and members of the public who are disabled access to information that is comparable to that of employees and members of the public without disabilities" (Section 508, 1998, 2005). Heumann and Seelman (1999) reported "the U.S. Department of Education … interpreted Section 508 to have application to state entities including some public colleges and universities" (as cited in Edmonds, 2004a, p. 53). Several states, most notably Illinois, Kansas, and Texas, have adopted laws like Section 508, which also have direct implications for higher education. Many institutions, recognizing the importance of providing accessibility to their students, have adopted policies based on Section 508. The University of Wisconsin–Madison (http://babel.lss.wisc.edu/access) and Oregon State University (http://tap.oregon-state.edu/508brief.htm) are notable examples.

Section 508 has unique importance as it provides precise guidelines and rules for electronic and information technology that directly addresses websites and other materials commonly used for online education. Section 508 is often used as the measure to determine if a resource is deemed accessible. Public institutions must show that their online courses, websites, and learning objects comply with Section 508.

The push to make Web pages accessible has not come from governmental authorities alone. The World Wide Web consortium (W3C) published its Web Content Accessibility Guidelines 1.0 in 1999, which also specifies from a Web-standards perspective how to make Web-based content accessible. Most Web developers will try to adhere to both Section 508 and W3C specifications, thereby creating pages that can be labeled as 508/W3C compliant. UseableNet is one vendor that offers accessibility and usability software solutions for the creation of text-based transcription of websites. The UsableNet LIFT products, currently used by over 100 higher education institutions, allow simple retrofitting of existing Web pages. All LIFT applications provide Section 508 and compliance.

Even though CMS systems such as Blackboard and WebCT are Section 508 compliant, online courses may still present barriers for disabled students (Edwards, 2003). The inclusion of noncompliant learning objects is one specific concern. Other concerns center on the reference or linking to third-party materials that may not be Section 508 compliant but that represent critical steps for the understanding of the lesson material. Online education administrators should work with faculty and course designers to raise awareness of the importance for Section 508 compliance and provide assistance with modifying existing course content.

Appointing an instructional designer or course designer to act as a compliance expert is a good practice. The accessibility expert assists and educates faculty/course developers on proper design techniques while reviewing all material prior to publication. This individual will also work as a liaison between online education and the institution's accessibility officer, further ensuring congruence with broader institutional policy.

Creation of accessible websites does more than assist physically challenged students; Nielsen (2000) argues that creating accessible course websites benefits all users. Capacities such as in-page text searching, ability to view captions, or the capacity to view content on low-resolution devices such as cell phones and PDAs (personal digital assistants) are all secondary benefits to accessible website design.

Table 5.11.   Accessibility Resources

Website Accessibility Guidelines:
- U.S. Department of Health and Human Services: http://www.Usability.gov
- Website Accessibility Initiative: http://www.w3.org/WAI/
- Electronic and Information Technology Accessibility Standards: http://www.access-board.gov/sec508/508standards.htm
- World Wide Web Consortium's Web Content Accessibility Guidelines 1.0: http://www.w3.org/TR/WAI-WEBCONTENT/

Website Accessibility Resources:
- *Providing Access to Students with Disabilities in Online Distance Education: Legal, Technical and Practical Considerations* by Curtis D. Edmonds (2003). Available online at the Center for Distance Learning Research (http://www.cdlr.tamu.edu/dec_2003/decProceedings/7-Edmunds-Providing%20Access%20to%20Students%20with%20Disabilities1.pdf)
- Distance Education: Access Guidelines for Students with Disabilities—California Community Colleges: http://www.htctu.net/publications/guidelines/distance_ed/disted.htm
- Information Technology and Disabilities E-Journal: http://www.rit.edu/~easi/itd.htm

Accessibility Resource Portal:
- University of Toronto Special Needs Opportunity Windows Courseware Accessibility Resources (SNOW): http://snow.utoronto.ca/access/courseware/index.html

Web Page Creation Tools:
- USablenet.com: http://www.usablenet.com
- Bobby: http://bobby.watchfire.com/bobby/html/en/index.jsp
- A-Prompt: http://www.aprompt.ca
- Temple University's WAVE Accessibility Tool: http://wave.webaim.org/index.jsp

Online Courses for Accessible Web Design:
- Equal Access to Software and Information (EASI) Online Courses and the Certificate in Accessible Information Technology: http://easi.cc/workshop.htm
- WebCT: http://www.webct.com/standards/viewpage?name=standards_accessibility

Selected University Sites:
- Accessibility in Distance Education—A Resource for Faculty in Online Teaching—UMUC—Accessibility in Distance Education: http://www.umuc.edu/ade
- University of Toronto Adaptive Technology Resource Center (ATRC)—Accessible Web-Based Distance Education: Principles and Best Practices: http://www.utoronto.ca/atrc/rd/library/papers/accDistanceEducation.html
- Web Accessibility Learning Modules—CSU Fresno: http://www.csufresno.edu/webaccess/learningmodules
- Michigan Virtual University Accessibility Standards for Quality Online Courses: http://standards.mivu.org/standards/access/

Course developers, seeking to develop accessible material, have numerous Web-based resources available that assist with creating accessable course materials. Useability.gov, Web Accessibility In Mind (WebAIM), W3C's Website Accessibility Initiative, Temple's WAVE Accessibility tool,

A-Prompt, and Bobby are among the most notable. Along with documentation and tutorials, these sites offer software, Web page scanning, and assistance to addressing specific problems in site design. For example, fully online courses are available from WebCT and Equal Access to Software and Information (EASI). There are also a number of outstanding papers, seminars, and conferences for Web developers that offer information and skills in creating accessible materials.

CHAPTER 6

ONLINE STUDENT SUCCESS

*The quality of a university is measured more by the
kind of student it turns out than the kind it takes in.*

—Robert J. Kibbee

As online education matures, researchers are learning more about which
elements promote online student success and which elements do not.
Since online student retention and course completion remain top issues
(O'Brien & Renner, 2002), institutions should take action to ensure students are both capable and equipped to succeed. Student success is
directly affected by administrative actions and policy. Institutions seeking
methods to increase online student success should focus on understanding the factors that influence online student retention while simultaneously providing appropriate preassessments, technical assessments,
and orientation courses.

ONLINE STUDENT RETENTION

Many early online programs suffered from alarmingly high dropout rates.
Lynch (2001) cites drop rates as high as 35% to 50%. O'Brien and Renner
(2002) note that student attrition remains a problem in online education.
These disturbing statistics caused more than a few to question the validity
of online education and many educators suggest that this is simply to be
expected in the online environment.

An Administrator's Guide to Online Education, 107–115
Copyright © 2005 by Information Age Publishing
All rights of reproduction in any form reserved.

We, however, do not believe the online "learning environment" is the cause nor do we agree that the "type" of students who enroll are predisposed to dropping. There are many online courses and programs that have little to no attrition (Council for Adult and Experiential Learning [CAEL], 2004; O'Brien & Renner, 2002, Shelton, 2004). Furthermore, examination from McVay (2000), Menager-Beeley (2001), O'Brien and Renner (2002), Moore, Bartkovich, Fetzner, and Ison (2002), Simpson (2003), CAEL (2004), and Dupin-Bryant (2004) point to specific factors that contribute to lower retention rates.

Student retention, in a wider institutional setting, has been researched extensively. For the most part, many of the same factors that influence retention in a face-to-face setting still hold true of online students (Simpson, 2003). In analyzing the current research derived from Menager-Beeley (2001), O'Brien and Renner (2002), Moore and colleagues (2002), CAEL (2004), and Dupin-Bryant (2004) addressing online education specifically, the following factors have emerged:

- Busy lives outside of school (Moore et al., 2002)
- Internet applications training (Dupin-Bryant, 2004)
- Lack of access to computers (Moore et al., 2002)
- Lack of experience in higher education in general (Moore et al., 2002)
- Lack of experience with online education (Moore et al., 2002)
- Large courseload (Moore et al., 2002)
- Low class rank (Dupin-Bryant, 2004)
- Low cumulative grade point averages (Dupin-Bryant, 2004)
- Low prior grades in English (Menager-Beeley, 2001)
- Low task values (Menager-Beeley, 2001)
- Number of previous courses completed online (Dupin-Bryant, 2004)
- Older students (over 28 years) (Menager-Beeley, 2001)
- Operating systems and file management training (Dupin-Bryant, 2004)
- Prior computer training (Dupin-Bryant, 2004)
- Prior educational experience (Dupin-Bryant, 2004)
- Searching the Internet training (Dupin-Bryant, 2004)
- Young age (under 25) (Moore et al., 2002)

Factors that have not shown to be influential:

- Ethnicity (Menager-Beeley, 2001; Moore et al., 2002)

- Gender (Menager-Beeley, 2001; Moore et al., 2002)
- Subject level of prior English class (Menager-Beeley, 2001)
- ESL (English as a Second Language) (Menager-Beeley, 2001)

Factors that have shown to positively influence retention are:

- Addressing safety and security needs to support highly interactive experiences (O'Brien & Renner, 2002)
- Close faculty/expert teamwork, consistent revision of courses (CAEL, 2004)
- Course content related to everyday work of working students (CAEL, 2004)
- Creating a sensitive online faculty persona (O'Brien & Renner, 2002)
- Enhancing the comfort level of students with the technology (O'Brien & Renner, 2002)
- Forced placement/screening test for students (CAEL, 2004)
- Institutionalwide commitment (CAEL, 2004)
- Instructor-led courses (not self-paced) (CAEL, 2004)
- Less than 20:1 student–faculty ratio (CAEL, 2004)
- Online orientation course (CAEL, 2004)
- Supplemental grant funding for student support services (CAEL, 2004)

Although there appears to be some mixed results (e.g., age), these studies do show several recurring commonalities. Of particular interest are the factors that are institutionally controlled. Institutions will never have complete control over retention, students will always have emergencies, and not every student will succeed. However, institutions can take a proactive approach in establishing what Simpson (2003) calls a retention-friendly institution. The first step is to formulate a retention strategy. Simpson proposes eight stages to follow in developing a retention strategy:

1. Define retention terms and prioritize them
2. Set targets for retention
3. Identify the vulnerable students
4. Design a system of early integrative contacts from the institution
5. Design a system of retention contacts to retain students on course
6. Design a system of retrieval and reclamation contacts
7. Restructure courses for retention
8. Restructure the institution for retention. (p. 150)

Table 6.1.   Student Retention Resources

- Calhoun Community College—OLE Project: http://www.calhoun.cc.al.us/distancelearning/ole/
- Center for the Study of College Student Retention: http://www.cscsr.org/
- National Academic Advising Association (NACADA): http://www.nacada.ksu.edu/Clearinghouse/AdvisingIssues/retain.htm
- Student Retention Center at UCLA: http://www.studentretentioncenter.ucla.edu
- The University of Oklahoma Outreach Consortium for Student Retention Data Exchange: http://www.ou.edu/csrde/index.html

One of the most effective tools for understanding attrition in a course or program is administrating a drop survey (Simpson, 2003). This survey should be routinely administered to all students immediately upon withdrawal (passively or actively) from a course. In some cases, a reclamation plan can be implemented, bringing that student back into the course immediately or during the next offering.

Simpson (2003) believes, as many other studies suggest, that there is a "clear link between qualifications on entry and dropout rates" (p. 11). Appropriately screening students for both academic and technical aptitude is clearly a necessary step to increasing course completion rates. Institutions, seeking to maximize student retention, should develop preassessment measures, technical assessment measures, and online orientation courses.

Student Preassessment

The selection of students who participate in the online program is important, as evidenced from the many studies addressing student retention. In fact, Buchanan (1999) suggests that preassessment ensures the validity of the program. Not only does preassessment help provide validity but it also decreases frustration levels for all involved. Buchanan further asserts that "to ignore such pre-assessment measures is to lessen the quality, pedagogical integrity, and learning experiences for all involved" (¶ 22).

The benefits of performing preselection assessments include:

- Minimal interruptions in the online classroom from students who consistently need assistance to accomplish the required tasks.
- Minimal need for student support.
- Decreased attrition.

- Identification of students who need to obtain or improve basic skills.
- Students proceed with confidence.

For the most part, the assessment of academic preparation occurs separate from the duties of the online program. Academic aptitude is, however, just one aspect that influences student effectiveness. Student selection should be addressed in two additional areas: student characteristics and technical competencies.

Wedemeyer (as cited in Keegan, 1996) recognized that distance education should not be considered for all students and this should include online education. The list below, as adapted from Buchanan (1999) and Northern Arizona University (2003), suggests the following characteristics are found in successful online students:

- Ability to articulate themselves in written form
- Ability to work in a collaborative environment
- Assertiveness
- Comfort with technology
- Commitment
- Goal-oriented
- Independence
- Involved
- Maturity
- Motivated
- Organization and management skills
- Self-discipline

Unfortunately, simply administering standardized aptitude test does not identify these traits. Recognition of these characteristics requires care-

Table 6.2.   List of Student Self-Evaluation Instruments

- Barstow College—Are Online Courses Right for You?: http://www.bcconline.com/cgi-bin/sfesurvey.cgi?areonlinecoursesrightforyou
- Great Basin College—Self-Evaluation for Potential Online Students: http://faculty.gbcnv.edu/onlinestudentsurvey.htm
- Portland Community College—Are Online Courses for Me?: http://www.distance.pcc.edu/orientation/mod1/mod1_quiz.cfm
- UCLA Self Assessment: http://www.onlinelearning.net/ole/holwselfassess.html
- University of Illinois—Self-Evaluation Tool for Potential Online Students: http://www.ion.uillinois.edu/resources/tutorials/pedagogy/selfEval.asp

ful self-examination from the student. To help facilitate this examination, many online programs have provided an inventory like the popular "Is Online Learning for Me?" assessment or a similar instrument to help students determine if they have the ability to be effective online learners. These instruments are usually placed online and made publicly available for potentially interested students.

Technical Assessment

Online education students must interact with technology. Not all students are comfortable interacting in a technology-rich environment, which may negatively impact learning and confidence. Beard, Harper, and Riley (2004) suggest that students who lack technical skills dread learning with technology. Technical assessments provide students with the confidence that they are capable of participating successfully, or in cases where they are not capable, recommends remediation. The technical assessment also assures the faculty and institution that all students enrolled in the online course have met minimum proficiency standards. Technical assessment is often broken down into two categories: assessments of students' computer systems and technical skills.

The students' computer must be capable of connecting to and interacting with the institution's servers. At a minimum, students must be informed of the basic computer requirements needed to participate in the online program. This can be accomplished by simply publishing a list of basic requirements analogous to the specs found on consumer-targeted software. On the other extreme, it may be as complex as an automated system that checks the user's computer automatically.

Several institutions use an automated or semi-automated computer system assessment like Northern Arizona University's WebCT System Compatibility Test (http://www2.nau.edu/ctel/preparing/sys_req/test/index.htm). In these types of systems, users navigate through a series of pages where software automatically checks browser plug-ins and performs hardware and network speed tests. The advantage of an automated system is users are only presented with activities when their systems do not meet the minimum requirements.

Institutions also need to assess students' technical skills. Again, the institution should, at a minimum, publish the technical skills required but may take a more active approach that would allow students to perform self-assessments or assisted assessments to ascertain if they possess the technical skills needed. The University of North Carolina at Chapel Hill offers their instructors a Customizable Online Skills Test (http://cf.unc.edu/skill-stest/create). Instructors are able to select from a list of proficiencies to cre-

Table 6.3.   List of Technical Skills Instruments

- Barstow College—Do You Need to Take Intro to Online Courses?: http://www.
  bcconline.com/cgi-bin/sfesurvey.cgi?doyouneedtotakeintrotoonlinecourses
- College of DuPage—Technical Skills Self-Assessment: http://www.cod.edu/Online/
  techskllr4.htm
- University of North Carolina—Technical Skills Assessment: http://www.sph.unc.edu/
  toolbox/skills_test.htm

ate a customizable skills assessment for students that matches the specific technical needs of the course.

In any of the assessments, failure should not be a permanent disqualification but an opportunity for the student to correct the problem and move forward. Materials, information, or tutoring should be provided for students to improve their skills.

Orientation Courses

Orientation courses are helpful for all stakeholders in online education. Not only do they play a significant role in student effectiveness (McVay, 2000), they reduce the need for technical support and help increase course completion rates. Orientation courses also play an important role in faculty satisfaction. Berge (2001) notes, "Instructors have a right to expect that participants will come to distance learning experiences prepared to study effectively at a distance" (p. 20).

Online education is fundamentally different from traditional education in the way that information is disseminated and how students interact with each other and the instructor (Willis, 1993). Students who are also adapting to new roles may need assistance in learning how to participate (McPherson & Baptista Nunes, 2004). Even among experienced students, programs at different institutions may have small differences in approach.

Institutions often provide an online orientation course as a way to introduce the concept of online learning. Orientation courses provide an experimental area where students can gain firsthand experience in online learning and thus make more informed decisions regarding how online education fits their personal learning styles.

There are two methods to providing orientation courses. The first approach allows students to receive actual course materials (often in a simplified presentation), view the syllabus, and the course calendar. Simpson (2003) notes that these are sometimes called samplers, test drives, taster packs, or course previews. Abilene Christian University provides students with a Sneak-a-peek-week prior to the official course start date. Each course includes a Module Zero that provides a sample of the course materials, thus giving students a glimpse of the course delivery method and assessments. The second approach is to create a fully separate and standalone online orientation course. This type of course usually provides an overview of online learning structures and helps students obtain the skills needed to be successful. Several institutions have taken this course to the credit level, offering one or more credit hours upon completion. These two approaches are not mutually exclusive; in fact, they may be best used together to provide a high-level overview regarding study skills and detailed information for specific courses.

The literature suggests important elements to include in orientation courses. The following list, compiled from our own experience and material from McVay (2000), Simpson (2003), and Bozarth, Chapman, and LaMonica (2004), provide an overview of the elements most often included in an orientation course. Interestingly, Bozarth and colleagues, surveying the perceived need for materials in orientation courses, reported that "while instructors focused heavily on the need for stronger technology skills, the student responses dealt almost entirely with issues of time management, personal commitment, and the need for realistic expectations" (p. 102).

Orientation courses should provide students with an understanding in how to:

- Log in to the courseware management system or website
- Logically navigate through the course
- Take online exams or assessments

It should provide examples of:

- Learning modules
- Learning objects
- A course calendar
- Assessment methods
- Discussion board or other asynchronous activities

It should offer:

- Technological training
- Tips for online study practices
- Time management strategies
- Overviews of pedagogical approaches and learning theories
- Links to resources and study materials for online learners

Table 6.4.   Orientation Courses Examples

- Fayetteville State University: http://www.uncfsu.edu/bb/students/docs/orientation.htm
- Illinois Valley Community College: http://www.ivcc.edu/eng1001/orientation/ policies.htm
- Laramie County College: http://de.lccc.cc.wy.us/disted/online/orientation/orient.htm
- Waubonsee Community College: http://www2.wcc.cc.il.us/public/orientation/

It should help the student:

- Become technically capable of completing an online course
- Become self-aware of the suitability of their leaning style
- Make adjustments that will lead to successful study
- Reflect upon online learning and their needs

Orientation courses are usually created with little expense, yet provide a significant benefit for the prospective student. A 2002 study by Hawksley and Owen in the United Kingdom found that 76% of students who were able to view examples of a course found it helpful. The Council for Adult and Experiential Learning (2004) lists an online orientation course first in its list of factors contributing to high completion rates. Lynch (2001) discovered, after implementing an orientation course at one university, the following outcomes:

- Eighty-nine percent of students entering the online program demonstrated a significant increase in technology skills following the completion of the orientation course.
- Seventy-four percent of students indicated an increase in independent, self-directed learning.
- Ninety-four percent of students were able to discern their preferred learning styles and to provide an accommodation plan, if needed, to be successful in the online environment.
- Ninety-five percent of students demonstrated an ability to communicate effectively using Web-based tools.
- The attrition rate of online students was reduced to an average of 15% and reenrollment increased to 90% (¶ 8).[1]

NOTE

1. From "Effective Student Preparation for Online Learning," by Maggie McVay Lynch in *The Technology Source*, November/December 2001. Reprinted with permission of the publisher and author.

CHAPTER 7

TECHNOLOGY AND THE COURSEWARE MANAGEMENT SYSTEM

All the computers in the world won't make a difference without enthusiastic students,
skilled and committed teachers, involved and informed parents and a society that
underscores the value of lifelong learning.

—Bill Gates

Dependence upon technology is one of the greatest risks facing online education. This dependency develops into an intricate dance performed between those who maintain technology and those who employ it. The complexity of a modern Courseware Management System (CMS) and the related infrastructure can be daunting, yet providing a stable and functional learning environment is absolutely necessary. White and Weight (2000) aptly observe, "An online student prevented from logging on to the classroom is comparable to an onsite student driving up to an educational facility to find the doors locked. Being unable to reach an online classroom, for whatever reason, rates as an emergency that must be resolved quickly" (pp. 71-72).

Only in rare instances will the program administrator be involved with all of the day-to-day technical operations. Instead, they rely upon the highly specialized skills of the institution's IT staff. This chapter discusses the relationship between online education and information technology,

An Administrator's Guide to Online Education, 117–133

the importance of the helpdesk, the issues related to CMS selection and support, portals, and an overview of the various tools to support learning.

INFORMATION TECHNOLOGY

Technology specialists play a pivotal role in the success of online education as they must work to meet the challenges of a complex technical infrastructure. Technology specialist along with online education administrators, together, must share the common goal of service to students and faculty effectively and efficiently. Creating a stable and reliable technical infrastructure is essential as it influences learning (White & Weight, 2000), student satisfaction (Gibbons & Wentworth, 2002), and student retention (O'Brien & Renner, 2002).

Institutions use three approaches to meet the technical needs of online education. These approaches are:

1. Technology staff that report directly to Online Education;
2. Partnership between IT and Online Education
3. Outsourcing using an application service provider (ASP).

In the first approach, the online program has its own technology staff that report directly to the Director of Online Education. This provides Online Education, at least in some respects, with a degree of independence and autonomy. This structure also ensures that dedicated technical staff are responsive to the needs of the program through a direct reporting structure.

Unfortunately, this approach tends to suffer from a lack of depth in personnel and skill levels within the technology staff. If a technical position becomes vacant for an extended period of time, it places a much greater and disproportionate workload on the remaining personnel. The challenge of finding, managing, and training qualified technicians should also be considered.

Even with this approach, the program will still have substantial interactions with the central IT organization, as it will depend upon the institutional data network, student information system, and financial management system. These elements, which are critical to the functionality of the CMS, are typically administrated from a central IT organization.

The second approach is to form a close partnership between the online program and the institution's IT organization. The day-to-day operations for maintaining complex technological systems are realized without direct involvement from the Director of Online Education. Along with provision of services, IT administrators also assist in providing leadership in planning for the technological aspects of the program.

The effectiveness of this approach is dictated by the strength of the partnership. IT organizations are often overwhelmed with requests and there is always competition for priority. IT must understand the strategic importance of stable and reliable online infrastructure and be committed to ensuring that issues that affect online courses are addressed immediately.

Finally, the third approach is to outsource CMS support through an Application Service Provider (ASP). An ASP handles the day-to-day technical operations and provides network bandwidth. The ASP provider usually dedicates a server for the institution or houses the institution's server on their company's network. ASP services are not inexpensive; however, they may be significantly less than it would take to hire dedicated staff. Depending upon the existing IT workload, a client/vendor relationship may prove to be more responsive to the demands of the online program.

One of the biggest disadvantages of the ASP model is the removal of the CMS from the campus network. On-campus users, such as faculty and online administration staff, often have slower access than if the servers were local. Also, not all ASP vendors will support all course management systems, and not all CMS vendors offer ASP services. If an ASP solution is chosen, it may limit the possible options for the CMS.

Each has unique advantages and disadvantages; however, the choice will be most dependent upon the institution's culture, philosophies, and available personnel.

Technological Impact

The best approach to making an informed and appropriate decision to provide for the technical needs of the online education program is to determine the impact the online program will have on the existing IT infrastructure. The costs of outsourcing or hiring additional staff must be weighed against the additional demands the online program will place upon the current technology staff. The impact will not just be related to the installation and management of the CMS; there will be increased load on the network, and a greater demand of desktop support and helpdesk services.

Online education impacts server maintenance because most CMS systems will be used continuously. Backups and routine maintenance can be challenging. Taking the CMS offline for backups causes significant issues for online students. Even scheduled downtime may catch online students halfway through a test or at a critical point in posting a discussion board topic. There are strategies that address continuously active systems, but these are significantly more expensive and create a greater impact on the technology staff.

The online program generates network traffic, which may overwhelm existing Internet bandwidth. The IT department must be aware of how instructional material, especially rich media content such as movies or interactive learning objects, will be used. Many online program administrators often consider additional Internet bandwidth or redundant bandwidth as an important element for accessibility and reliability.

The IT helpdesk is also likely to experience increased demands from online faculty. Faculty who develop course content will often increase the need for support. Requests for faster computers, scanners, color printers, or video capture equipment are also common.

STUDENT HELPDESK

Online students, like instructors, require technical support. If an online student is unable to resolve technical problems, frustration and isolation will occur, which, in turn, will affect student retention and learning (McGorry, 2003). While faculty need assistance with technical issues themselves, more importantly, they need someone else to address the technical issues of their students. "Instructors cannot be responsible for other than cursory training of their students in the use of technology. The organization must bear the responsibility of basic educational technology training" (Miller & King, 2003, p. 292).

Since online students interact at all hours, helpdesk services should ideally be offered 24 hours a day, 7 days a week (Hitch & MacBrayne, 2003). However, provision of 24x7 support is challenging. In fact, Arabasz, Boggs, and Baker's (2003) research indicated that 71% of respondents rated 24/7 support as a challenge—second only to securing adequate funding to handle demand. No current data could be found to address the percentage of online programs that utilize a 24-hour helpdesk. However, the *U.S. News & World Report* Best of the Online Grad Programs (2001) survey of the 130 graduate online programs identified only 39 institutions (30%) that offered the helpdesk services on a 24-hour, 7-day-a-week basis.

Whenever possible, institutions should make student technical assistance available in an online format. Placing support online allows students to find access to the materials they need, when they need them without direct interaction with helpdesk staff. The self-service approach for technical support is one that takes fewer human resources and is available 24 hours a day. Appropriate documentation, FAQ's (Frequently

Asked Questions), and links to commonly needed software should be available for download.

Helpdesk services may be provided internally, through institutional staffing, or by outsourcing. Providing the helpdesk services for online learners internally is accomplished by assigning additional duties to the existing technology support office or by hiring additional staff that report directly to the Office of Online Education. If the institution chooses to outsource the helpdesk, there are solutions for outsourcing. SunGard Collegis, Inc. (http://www.sungardcollegis.com) and Embanet both offer outsourced helpdesk solutions for US-based institutions. Charges for their services are contingent upon the number of students anticipated per year. These services can be surprisingly cost effective when the cost of adding additional labor to an existing helpdesk is considered.

COURSEWARE MANAGEMENT SYSTEM

The Courseware Management System (CMS) is arguably the most important technological element for online education. It certainly is one of the most visible. (For an introduction to CMS applications and their use, refer to Table 7.1.) Because of the importance of the CMS in online education, a significant amount of attention needs to be given to selection and support. There is no greater technological decision in online education than that of the CMS.

CMS systems have become ubiquitous on college campuses within the past 10 years. A recent EDUCAUSE Core Date Services survey indicates that from the 621 institutions that responded, over 90% of campuses are using a CMS (Hawkins, Rudy, & Madsen, 2003). While that may be slightly skewed since EDUCAUSE is an organization seeking to serve technology-focused campuses, it provides ample evidence that the CMS is an important element for most institutions. The following section discusses the need to reevaluate CMS features, highlights a method for CMS selection, discusses evaluation of commercial, homegrown, and open source options, and spotlights the debate over commercial versus open source CMS support. A special overview of the Sakai Project follows.

CMS Feature Evaluation

Since faculty and students spend so much time interacting within the CMS, providing a rich and productive environment is vital. Struggling with an outdated or poorly matched CMS not only frustrates those who use the system, but effects learning outcomes (White & Weight, 2000).

Table 7.1.   CMS Primer

The courseware management system (CMS) is an online learning environment where students participate in their courses, interact with their instructors, and collaborate with their classmates. It is analogous to a virtual campus. It performs not only as the virtual classroom, but also as a student commons area, faculty office, and study center. A CMS is not just a single software application but a suite of tools that enables the delivery of online courses. The CMS allows content experts to create, edit, and deliver educational content online and usually includes assessment and gradebook applications. This suite of tools can be broken down into four categories: content management, collaboration/communication, testing/assessment, and administrative utilities.

Content management allows for the creation of content, editing of existing content, and the organization of Web pages, streamed audio/video, and server-based files. Collaboration and communication tools offer synchronous communication capabilities, such as a chat server, virtual whiteboards, along with asynchronous communication capabilities, such as course announcements, threaded discussions, email lists, and gradebook features. Testing and assessment features provide online testing mechanisms, tools for online test creation, and a grading system. Finally, administrative utilities facilitate the creation of course sections, the copying of course content, and CMS user management functions.

In recent years, CMS systems have added additional features to the basic classroom management tools, broadening their scope and utility. Portals, provided by the CMS vendor, are a popular option for CMS systems. Features such as electronic portfolios, file management, and media streaming are also available. CMS companies will continue to expand the capabilities of their products, bringing about new and innovative ways to offer online educational materials and facilitate courses.

The role the CMS plays in online education is largely consistent from one institution to another; however, there are widespread minor differences from course to course. Some instructors interact with students primarily asynchronously by posting lesson content and interacting with students in the discussion board over a given period of time. For institutions that use this method of instruction, the content management system and the class discussion tools will be the most valuable. Other institutions place more value on synchronous communication where faculty lecture and interact with students in real time. Institutions utilizing this mode of instruction will place greater emphasis on the chat server (text, audio, and even video) and tools such as a virtual whiteboard and shared web browser.

Ideally, a campus could simply change CMS vendors as CMS features evolve, institutional needs change, or as market trends dictate. Unfortunately, changing a component as central and pervasive as the CMS is to online education is an immense undertaking and one that mandates massive resources. Nevertheless, it can be done and online program administrators should keep abreast of advancements in CMS products.

The Dallas County Community College District (DCCCD), a system of seven community colleges in Dallas County, Texas, performs routine CMS evaluations every 3 years (E. Ramos, personal communication, November 5, 2003). Periodic evaluation, such as performed by the DCCCD, ensures all participants that their needs in a CMS are being evaluated and considered. This practice also allows administrators and technical staff to stay aware of changes throughout the marketplace.

When it comes to CMS features, some users may find value in a particular CMS tool, while others find that same tool frustrating and cumbersome. CMS licensing, server hardware, and related instructional technology resources are all costly. If left unchecked, there are no limits to what an institution could spend adding and supporting additional features and capabilities. Therefore, the institution should focus on the features that directly support the teaching and learning process and not on the bells and whistles.

Selection of the CMS

Selection of a CMS that meets the needs of a campus requires a thorough understanding of the features provided by the CMS. Competing products and overlapping features from numerous vendors can make the CMS comparisons difficult. Edutools.org, an independent website developed by the Western Cooperative for Educational Telecommunications (WCET), provides an excellent resource for narrowing the choice of competing CMS products. The Edutools approach is quite practical in its design and the interactive features are far better than anything we could describe in this book.

Edutools offers a wealth of information regarding CMS tools, including news and independent product evaluations. One of the most helpful features of the site is the CMS *Compare By Features* tool (http://edutools.org/course/compare/byfeatures/index.jsp). Administrators are able to interactively search for a CMS product based on features they select as necessary. The extensive database returns a list of all products that adhere to those specifications.

Faculty members' request for CMS features should play a large part in the purchasing decision. Ideally, administrators should allow faculty input into CMS selection. Taking the time to listen to faculty members' suggestions, and gaining the respect of faculty increases faculty buy-in and satisfaction. One notable approach was taken by Texas Woman's University which held a CMS fair and invited vendors to demonstrate their products. This created faculty awareness among the available CMS products.

Multiple CMS Systems

The EDUCAUSE Core Date Services survey that indicates 90% of institutions chose to implement a CMS also indicates that almost 10% of those institutions chose to implement multiple commercial course management systems (Hawkins et al., 2003). Continuing to support multiple CMS systems is a practice that should receive careful scrutiny. Whether formal, or informal, the decision should center on several areas: financial feasibility, support concerns, and student effectiveness.

A strong contributing factor for selecting a single CMS system is the cost involved in licensing multiple CMS systems. Commercial CMS systems such as Blackboard and WebCT cost many thousands of dollars each year. There is an additional indirect cost to maintain the technology. As technology budgets are stretched thinner each year, the money and time spent on support for multiple CMS systems could be better spent on the provision of additional features or services.

A single CMS allows for more focused support. Managing multiple CMS systems also necessitates redundancy in training and support. Course developers, support staff, the helpdesk, and other personnel who interact with online students or online faculty will need training on multiple systems. Orientation courses, support pages, and help documentation will also need to be duplicated.

Perhaps the strongest factor in favor of using a single CMS is the student. Students can learn in different CMS systems; the question is, should they be forced to? We believe students should not. Students should be provided with a consistent learning environment in order to maximize the focus on learning. Most students find comfort in consistency. Boettcher and Conrad (1999) and O'Brien and Renner (2002) recognized that students' comfort level with technology affects participation. Students should "focus on the learning and not be distracted by the underlying technology" (O'Brien & Renner, 2002, p. 1480). Obviously, multiple CMS systems provide more distractions than one; however, the extent to which it affects learning has not yet been shown.

Academe has long embraced experimentation and academic freedom. These ideals are the backbone of higher education. Without them, the concept of online education may have never evolved. However, institutions must decide if multiple CMS systems provide more value in the freedom of faculty choice, or the need to maximize support and capital resources into a single system.

Commercial CMS Systems

The 1990s saw a number of vendors competing for their share in a new CMS software market. The intoxication of dot.com wealth and the excitement of shaping a new market generated much enthusiasm. Some of the early CMS providers have grown and prospered, others have not. When the dust settled, two major players remained: Blackboard and WebCT.

These two now hold the lion's share of the market and directly compete with similar products and offerings. According to Market Data Retrieval (2005), Blackboard recorded the largest market share at 51% of colleges, followed by WebCT at 32%. Blackboard recently went public and is showing reasonable profitable performance. WebCT, a privately held company, offers little financial data but hinted at expectations of profitability in 2001 (Arnone, 2001).

Both of these vendors license their products annually and price is generally based upon the total student full time equivalency (FTE) of the entire institution. The cost of licensing these products has risen sharply in the past several years and may continue to do so (Young, 2002a). This increase in cost has become a critical issue at many institutions and is one of the major reasons why many are being forced to reexamine their choice of CMS platform.

Viable alternatives to Blackboard and WebCT are available in the marketplace. While these alternative companies are much smaller in market share and capitalization, they do have products that offer similar features and, in some cases, are more advanced. Penn State's World Campus, among others, has successfully used Angel, a product of CyberLearningLabs. Desire2Learn Inc. has recently experienced success with its standards-based architecture as it replaced both Blackboard and WebCT for University of Minnesota State Colleges and Universities and the University of Wisconsin System. Unicon Academus, Intralearn, and FirstClass are additional CMS solutions that have found their place among respected institutions and offer similar tools for online course delivery. The long-term sustainability of these companies is a risk that should be considered, but as history has shown, today's innovators can often be tomorrow's market leaders.

Other competitors in the CMS market have taken a different approach, focusing on bundling of services rather than strictly the licensing of software. Two noteworthy vendors, eCollege and The Learning House, offer complete solutions for the institution. Fee structures, typically based per student, help pay for premium services such as helpdesk and consultation.

Homegrown CMS Systems

The EDUCAUSE Core Date Services survey reported that fewer than 6% of its respondents employed a homegrown CMS (Hawkins et al., 2003). There are substantial risks as well as rewards for utilizing a homegrown CMS solution. While institutions are able to create systems that are customized to their exact needs, they also place themselves in a position to maintain and support the CMS indefinitely. Deploying a homegrown CMS is a significant commitment of resources, but the rising cost of commercial systems provides some comfort that the institution at least has direct control over CMS expenses.

Open Source CMS Systems

Open source software offers a balance between a homegrown CMS and commercial alternatives. Once installed and configured, it provides a product that is ready to use. Unlike a commercial CMS, the open source license provides the institution with both the source code and the authorization to modify the product as it chooses. The Sakai Project (see "Sakai Project" later in this chapter) has brought an increased focus on the validity of open source CMS solutions. While Sakai is not a CMS, it does offer a framework for implementing several open source CMS tools, ensuring interoperability between those CMS products and various other academic support software packages.

Open source software is a concept whereby the source code is made freely available and the end user has the right to modify and redistribute the software as they see fit. Software in the open source model is not supported by any single propriety source, but among a distributed network of developers (both individuals and organizational) who freely contribute to its advancement. According to Wikipedia, the open source movement is based on the belief that distributing support among collective individuals yields software that is more reliable, stable, and secure than software that is produced among a smaller, less diverse group of developers working in a single company. Robinson (2005) likens the open source development process to the academic peer review process. He claims, "Just like the peer review process leads to high-quality scholarly and scientific work, peer scrutiny produces high-quality open source software" (p. 52).

OKI

The Open Knowledge Initiative (OKI) is an important standard relating to open source software which (http://www.okiproject.org/) originated at Massachusetts Institute of Technology in 2001. According to their website (http://www.okiproject.org), OKI "develops specifications that describe how the components of an educational software environment communicate with each other and with other enterprise systems." OKI publishes specifications, called OKI Service Interface Definitions (OSIDs), which specify how various CMS components interoperate. CMS systems that comply with standards give institutions the ability to choose functional modules a la carte from various sources. Three of the most prominent software initiatives working toward OKI compliance are MIT's Stellar (http://stellar.mit.edu/), Stanford University's CourseWork (http://www.stanford.edu/group/ats/coursework/), and the University of Michigan's CHEF project. These open source CMS solutions and their representative institutions are now core to the development of the Sakai Project.

The Great Support Debate

The institution's need for CMS support becomes both a fundamental and strategic decision. Assuming that the features of open source CMS systems and commercial systems will stay relatively competitive, the deciding factor for migrating to an open source CMS for many institutions will be based upon support. The question of support for the Sakai Project was identified as a primary concern at the July 2004 Syllabus conference (Blaisdell, 2005). Victor Edmonds, director of the University of California at Berkeley's Educational Technology Services, responded by calling into question similar concerns with Blackboard and WebCT's CMS support (as cited in Blaisdell, 2005).

Mara Hancock, associate director of the University of California at Berkeley's Learning Systems and Multimedia Services, proposes a three-category model for evaluating support between competing CMS products (as cited in Blaisdell, 2005). Her model focuses on frontline customer support, technical support, and implementation support. Following Hancock's model, institutions should evaluate what services are available in each category and weigh those together to make an informed opinion on support needs.

Commercial CMS providers offer support as a part of their yearly licensing fees. Additional levels of support are often negotiable as services such as turnkey installation and other assistance are available on a professional services contract basis. Unfortunately, it appears from reading the listservs that some institutions are not satisfied with the support they are getting from Blackboard and WebCT.

Open source software brings a new perspective on support. In fact, institutions can choose to support the software themselves or contract for support from a number of independent companies. For example, commercial support for the Sakai Project is provided from the Sakai Commercial Affiliates (SCA), for-profit companies that offer support for the Sakai Project's community source software (http://www.sakaiproject.org/support.html). The fact that no single company controls the direction of the software is, however, a disadvantage for some. The Sakai movement currently has strong leadership among a consortium of universities and other organizations who are overseeing its development. However, the question of future support and improvements to the software worry administrators (Fuchs, 2004).

Integrating the CMS

The decision to integrate the CMS with existing campus information systems is significant. Integration with campus databases allows automating many of the tasks involved in managing the online program, such as course creation, population of students into courses, and even submission of final grades. It does, however, involve significant effort from IT to provide the integration.

Manual processes tend to lead to human error, delays in data input, and lack of uniformity across the data. Manual data entry also takes time to perform, which leads to higher personnel costs. The desire to minimize errors, reduce cost, and automate many of the more monotonous tasks in online course management drives the justification for a fully integrated CMS.

The integration of the CMS is neither easy nor inexpensive. Most CMS vendors address the integration issue by providing a system that has documented application program interfaces (API) that allow for the integration of the CMS to the institutional Student Information System (SIS). This, however, only provides for the ability to integrate, not the actual program to perform the integration, which must be either developed by the institution's programmers or by purchasing professional services provided by the CMS vendor and/or outside consultants. Depending on the SIS used and the CMS purchased, these professional services can range in the tens of thousands of dollars for a fully integrated system. Furthermore, many of the CMS vendors have placed a premium on the systems with documented APIs and often charge three to four times more in annual licensing fees for these systems than for a system that cannot be integrated.

Campus culture will dictate the amount of automation and integration expected. Some institutions routinely provide faculty with stock installations of systems and expect faculty to learn and manage the systems on their own. For other institutions, faculty expectations suggest a much more supportive process. While the decision may be heavily influenced by funding and human resources available to accomplish the task, the need to provide a seamless learning environment for faculty and students should be heavily considered.

PORTAL

A portal is a website or Web-based application that allows access to other websites or Web-based applications. In online education, the portal provides the interface to the CMS and/or other Web-based software. It also provides students with links to the specific online courses in which he or she has enrolled, and may also provide access to registration systems and student support services such as the library or the bookstore.

Single sign-on is a feature generally offered with a portal. Single sign-on passes authentication information from the portal to other Web-based applications, allowing access without reauthentication by the user. Single sign-on benefits the student, providing the convenience of authenticating only once for numerous systems. It benefits the institution because students are less likely to need helpdesk support in changing or resetting multiple passwords.

Web-based applications that can be integrated into a portal are increasing. Instructional software continues to be developed and adopted at a swift pace. Applications that show particular interest for online education are:

- Collaborative Work Tools—Tools that allow group collaboration over the Internet.
- Content Management—Tools that facilitate the creation and management of Web pages and websites.
- Electronic Portfolio—Tools that allow users to display electronic/digital materials used for assessment to selected audiences.
- Digital Repository—A collection of materials stored in a digital format with corresponding meta-data.
- File Management Tools—Tools that facilitate the management of files across the network.
- Plagiarism Prevention—Software that scans documents for plagiarized material.
- Weblog (Blog)—Web-based journaling software.
- Online Library Reserve—Software that provides reserve materials to students.

TOOLS TO SUPPORT LEARNING

Learning objects, defined by Wiley (2002) as "any digital resource that can be reused to support learning" (p. 6), are widely used in online education. The creation of learning objects and learning materials for online courses require technological tools. Online program administrators are often tasked with overseeing their creations, managing their usage, and supporting their deployment.

Authoring/creative tools, such as Adobe Photoshop, Macromedia Flash, and Microsoft PowerPoint, are widely used to create online learning materials. There are also more specific tools that have been uniquely created for online education and higher education. These can be loosely grouped into two major categories:

Learning Object Authoring
- Anystream: Apreso (http://www.anystream.com/)
- Design Science: WebEQ (http://www.dessci.com)
- Elluminate: Elluminate Live (http://www.elluminate.com/)
- Giunti Interactive Labs: learn exact (http://www.learnexact.com/)
- HorizonWimba: Live Classroom, EduVoice, and WebLab (http://www.horizonwimba.com)
- Impactica: Impactica for PowerPoint, Impatica OnCue (http://www.impatica.com/)
- The Learning Edge: LCMS (http://www.thelearningedge.com.au)
- Link-Systems International: NetTutor (http://www.link-systems.com/)
- RealObjects: edit-on Pro (http://www.realobjects.com/)
- Tech Smith: Camtasia Studio (http://www.techsmith.com)
- Tegrity: WebLearner (http://www.tegrity.com/)
- Trivantis: Lectora (http://www.trivantis.com/)

Testing and Assessment
- Brownstone Research Group, Inc.: Diploma Campus EDU Campus (http://www.brownstone.net/)
- Questionmark: Questionmark Perception (http://www.questionmark.com)
- Respondus: Respondus (http://www.respondus.com/)
- Software Secure: Securexam (http://www.softwaresecure.com/)

Creating learning objects and materials involves a significant investment of time and labor. Many institutions and course developers have offered to share their materials with others. Several websites, such as Multimedia Educational Resource for Learning and Online Teaching (MERLOT), host large collections of learning objects and may even provide peer reviews and assessments. The following is a list of additional Learning Object Repositories:

- Adult Learning Activities (http://www.cdlponline.org)/
- Apple Learning Interchange (http://ali.apple.com/ali/)
- Campus Alberta Repository of Educational Objects (http://careo.netera.ca)
- The Connexions Project at Rice University (http://cnx.rice.edu)
- EOE Foundation Java Applet Library (http://www.eoe.org/eoe.html)
- Gateway to Educational Materials (GEM) Project (http://www.thegateway.org/)
- Learning About Learning Objects: (http://www.learning-objects.net/modules.php?name=Web_Links)
- The Maricopa Learning eXchange (MLX) (http://www.mcli.dist.maricopa.edu/mlx/)
- Massachusetts Institute of Technology's Open Course Ware Initiative (http://ocw.mit.edu/index.html)
- Mid-South Community College (http://learn.midsouthcc.edu/)
- Multimedia Educational Resource for Learning and Online Teaching (MERLOT) (http://www.merlot.org)
- SMETE (http://www.smete.org/smete/)
- Wisconsin Online Resource Center (http://www.wisc-online.com/index.htm)

Learning Object Standards

A set of standards to ensure the interoperability and reusability of learning objects between various learning management systems now exists. For the most part, course developers do not need to know the details of these standards; however, they do need to have a general understanding of these standards to make informed decisions on the purchasing of learning materials. The two most prominent standards related to learning materials are IMS and SCORM.

IMS

IMS (once called Instructional Management Systems, but now known exclusively as IMS) standards are promoted by the IMS Global Learning Consortium, Inc. (http://www.imsglobal.org/). The IMS is a consortium of over 50 "hardware and software vendors, educational institutions, publishers, government agencies, systems integrators, multimedia content providers, and other consortia" that support "the adoption and use of learning technology" (IMS Global Learning, 2005). IMS members work together to create standards related to exchanging learning content and

Table 7.2.   IMS Resources

- A list of organizations that support IMS standards is located at: http://www. imsglobal.org/imsSpecAdoption.pdf
- A list of products that comply with IMS standards is located at: http://www.imsglobal.org/ direct/getproducts.cfm

---

user information within learning components. There are currently 15 IMS standards.

Learning content that is IMS compliant provides portability between various learning systems from different vendors. Purchasing and developing learning materials that are IMS compliant reduces the risk of being locked into one specific CMS, as the materials are transportable to another system. One of the greatest advantages of the IMS standards are for commercial learning content creators who now have the ability to develop for a single standard rather than numerous proprietary CMS formats.

SCORM

In online education, Sharable Courseware Object Reference Model (SCORM) is the "reference model that defines the interrelationship of course components, data models and protocols so that learning content objects are sharable across systems that conform with the same model" (Implementing ADL, 2003). The United States Federal Government created SCORM in 1999 and required all request for proposals for training with the Armed Services to be SCORM compliant (Scorm 1.2 Business, 2004). SCORM 1.2 currently combines AICC API (Appendix B) specification with the IMS 1.1 or 1.2 content packaging specifications (Scorm 1.2, 2003). SCORM is now a subset of standards within IMS. SCORM was initially designed to allow for interchangeable and reusable learning materials. While institutional instructional designers have little to do with creating SCORM-compliant materials, they should understand the importance of this standard when looking for prepackaged online learning materials, especially if they seek to provide educational materials to the U.S. military.

SAKAI PROJECT

The Sakai Project, a partnership between the University of Michigan, Indiana University, Massachusetts Institute of Technology, Stanford University, and the uPortal consortium (http://www.sakaiproject.org), has sparked a great deal of interest across higher education. With an all-star roster and funding already approaching $7 million, it has significant presence. Factor in saving potentially thousands by replacing commercial software with the free software offered through the Sakai Project and there is a great potential for widespread adoption across higher education.

The Sakai Project is not a CMS, or even a portal, but it does provide the infrastructure for both and seeks to offer three major objectives:

- A framework that builds on the recently ratified JSR 168 portlet standard and the OKI open service interface definitions to create a services-based, enterprise portal for tool delivery.
- A refactored set of educational software tools that blends the best of features from the participants' disparate software (e.g., course management systems, assessment tools, workflow, etc.).
- A synchronization of the institutional clocks of these schools in developing, adopting, and using a common set of open source software.

The Sakai Project is built using the open source software model. While some open source software is some of the most stable software today, it does carry certain risks. These risks center on the provision of support and the lack of any single service provider who is financially compelled to provide support in a timely and competent manner. Many information technology experts suggest that the perceived support risks of open source software are not founded completely on fact (Robinson, 2005, p. 52). Proponents of open source often boast about the superiority of open source support to commercial support, but administrators may find it difficult to justify those assertions in a business plan.

As the open source movement expands, many companies are filling the support needs of open source software by providing commercial support. According to their website, the Sakai Project already lists four capable and well-known vendors under the Sakai Commercial Affiliates (SCA) program. These vendors provide expertise with hosting, consulting, installation, integration, and support services.

Sakai seeks to be completely self-sustaining by 2008 (Young, 2004). It already has a significant presence at four large research universities. Sakai's ability to capture market share from the commercial vendors remains to be seen. The potential of Sakai warrants close observation and should be considered a potential option when developing 5-year plans and long-range budgets.

CHAPTER 8

MARKETING THE
ONLINE PROGRAM

Doing business without advertising is like winking at a girl in the dark.
You know what you are doing, but nobody else does.

— Stuart Henderson Britt

Higher education has sometimes struggled with marketing academic programs. Robinson (2004) suggested that "it is not that no marketing takes place, only that it sometimes it is more of an afterthought than a carefully developed strategy" (p. 271). Rheingold (2001) suggests that those in academe may even be suspicious of marketing efforts. Nevertheless, students must be aware of the online program to enroll and those students must also have a positive perception of the institution and believe the online program will meet their needs. Some institutions, such as the for-profit University of Phoenix, are aggressive in marketing their program, and according to published reports, that marketing is paying off in enrollments. In fact, *The Chronicle of Higher Education* reported a dramatic increase in the University of Phoenix online program, from 16,000 students in 2000 to almost 50,000 students in 2002 (Olsen, 2002).

To many people, marketing is equated with advertising. Sergio Zyman, former chief operation officer for Coca-Cola, clearly differentiated marketing from advertising. He believed marketing was not advertising or a combination of advertising and other activities. According to Zyman (1999), marketing "is a strategic activity and a discipline focused on the

An Administrator's Guide to Online Education, 135–144
Copyright © 2005 by Information Age Publishing

endgame of getting more consumers to buy your product more often so that your company makes more money" (p. 80).

Institutions that successfully market their programs are seeing healthy enrollments (Carnevale & Olsen, 2003). The institution must, however, solidly commit to marketing the online program for a substantial period of time for these payoffs to be fully realized. Sustained marketing relies on a comprehensive marketing plan and that plan is dependent upon institutional leadership to provide focus to the online program's marketing strategy. Jeffrey Feldberg, CEO and co-founder of Embanet Corporation, prescribes that "the programs that are going to win are the ones that know how to effectively market themselves" (Lorenzo, 2002, ¶1).

Online education tells an interesting and exciting story that offers unique advantages and benefits to prospective students. Getting the story to prospective students is important. This chapter provides an overview of the marketing mix and how the communication to internal and external audiences takes place. Promotion, one element of the mix that many administrators question, is given greater discussion with an extended breakout on online marketing.

DEVELOPING A MARKETING STRATEGY

Each online education program should develop a marketing plan and procedure for implementation that fits within a prescribed budget. Obviously, it would be easy to develop a marketing plan if funds were unlimited (Robinson, 2004). But in academe, that is not usually the case. Lynnette Porter (1997), in *Creating the Virtual Classroom*, outlines a successful course of action for marketing the online program. She recommends developing the marketing plan in the following order: "evaluating the program, setting objectives, identifying personnel and equipment, analyzing the target audience, identifying your market role, and selecting media for marketing" (p. 184).

Use the Right Human Resources

Academic departments and marketing and public relations professionals should drive the marketing strategy. Nonprofit institutions can learn from the for-profits; a well-designed marketing campaign run by marketing professionals will bring in large enrollments. If budget allows, consider hiring a third-party firm or work with marketing representatives from a consortium to manage the promotion. Several reputable companies are available that will help higher education institutions formulate,

Table 8.1.   Procedure for Marketing an Online Education Program

A good marketing plan for online education consists of the following steps:

1. Conduct a situational analysis of the program (where it is now, how it got there, and where it is headed).

2. Establish marketing objectives that clearly specify the intended future direction of the program.

3. Map a marketing strategy that explains in detail how objectives will be met (what will be done, who will do it, when it will be done).

4. Analyze the target audience again (what appeals to them, what their needs are, etc.).

5. Determine the desirable market position (establish the program as a leader in business teleconferencing services; position the program as the only vendor in an online degree in a specific subject area; offer the lowest cost Web-based courses for adults within the region).

6. Determine the best media and advertising mix (use only print media throughout the year; plan a 50/50 mix of television and radio advertisements 3 weeks before a new term starts).

Note: Creating the Virtual Classroom: Distance Learning with the Internet, p. 184, by Lynette Porter, Copyright © 2000 Jossey-Bass Publishers. This material is used by permission of John Wiley & Sons, Inc.

implement, and maintain a marketing campaign, but the institution may pay anywhere from 20% to 30% of the promotion budget for the service.

Identify the Target Audience

Marketing is often described as being both internally and externally focused. There should be a strategic marketing focus of both internal and external audiences. The message that is delivered and the audiences to whom it is delivered will be different, but the importance is just as critical. The message, regardless of the audience, should be "clear, concise, professional, and targeted for the maximum effect at the lowest possible cost" (Robinson, 2004, p. 271).

Internal Audiences

Internal marketing is important during the creation of the online program and throughout its existence. The internal audience should be considered when selling the program to the institution and obtaining faculty buy-in. Once the program grows, internal marketing helps ensure the proper emphasis is given in the budgeting processes.

Within an institution of higher education, there are four internal audiences: administration, faculty, staff, and existing students. An institutional leader, who garners the respect of the four audiences, can begin to distribute the internal marketing message. That message should be echoed from other institutional leaders and continued until the program is established. Sevier (2002) observed that "people—especially internal audiences—love to be in the know, keeping them involved and informed puts them in a position of offering insight to and having influence with their peers" (p. 27).

External Audiences

Regardless of the methods used, the external marketing campaign should be conducted in a centralized approach to ensure the appropriate exposure is gained and the proper message is delivered. Identifying the audience of potential students is critical. Narrowing the focus is essential as online students can be adult or traditional, local or distant, degree seeking or non-degree seeking, undergraduate or postgraduate. The needs of online students are often just as varied. Charp (2000) states, "Typical distance learners are those who don't have access to programs, employees who work during scheduled class hours, homebound individuals, self-motivated individuals who want to take courses for self-knowledge or advancement, or those who are unable or unwilling to attend class" (p. 10). Others simply see online education as an interesting medium and appreciate the student-centered approach to education.

Strategic Marketing.   Marketing is a strategic activity (Zyman, 1999). Building on the program's goals will allow the marketing to be more directed and in line with long-term institutional objectives that were established in the strategic planning process. Carnevale and Olsen (2003) suggest, "A program that attracts and keeps students is also likely to rely on strong marketing and to remain close to the core mission of the institution behind it" (p. A31). The message should be focused on the long term. To keep the focus consistent over time, the institution should refer to the needs assessment and other information used in goal-setting activities.

Prospective students must be informed of what the online program can do for them and must believe that the program meets their perceived needs before they enroll. Many students lack the knowledge regarding online education and the benefits it adds to lifelong learning. These students must be convinced with both informative and persuasive messages over time.

Relationship of the Online Program to the Institution.   Online programs are often a small component within the broad scope of an institution. Because of that relationship, the online program will share a great deal of interdependence with the established image of the institution in the marketplace. Any message that the online program communicates that contradicts the established image of the institution will cause confusion within the marketplace and hurt both the online program and the institution it serves.

THE MARKETING MIX

McCarthy (1960) categorized the basic elements of the marketing mix: product, price, place, and promotion. These four elements have since become the basis for modern marketing. Following this example, the institution should examine the online program's value in each of these elements and craft a message that communicates that value.

Place

The element of place offers an interesting perspective on how to illustrate the value of the online education program to a potential student. For prospective students, having the ability to participate in education regardless of place is often of great value. The anytime, anyplace nature of online education is often one of the core marketing messages in online education. To a student who is deciding between online education and traditional education, or even other methods of distance education, place is often a deciding factor.

Conversely, because all online programs are equally accessible over the Internet, the element of place is sometimes removed when distinguishing one institution's online program from another. For many regional or community-based institutions, place is a cornerstone of their traditional marketing campaigns. These institutions must incorporate a new strategic approach to the way they market their online programs. If a prospective student is already sold on the concept of online education but have not yet decided on an institution, then another element in the marketing mix will be the deciding factor.

Product

Product is a major ingredient in defining the perceived value of an online program to a prospective student. An institution should identify what distinguishes the value their educational offerings have over other institutions' comparable offerings. The institution should also reevaluate this value in the context of the online program and look for similar distinctive differences. Projecting those differences should be a major priority of the marketing message.

Within the context of online education, the product element is a critical deciding factor for many students. Institutions that offer a "brand name" or a recognizable education have distinct advantages over "no-name" institutions within this element of marketing. To counter this perception, an institution should project its value and look for distinctive ways to fit into the marketplace.

Price

The element of price brings sharp comparisons to competing programs. Equal quality for a lower cost is perceived as valuable to a prospective student. If an institution's price is higher than other competitors, the marketing message should emphasize other factors and build upon overall value, not price alone.

Price is often an element that cannot be easily adjusted in traditional education. Price structures for online education, however, may be a bit more flexible. The ability for some institutions to set flat-rate tuition, provide in-state pricing for all students, or in some cases, set market-driven pricing provides greater flexibility to reach prospective students.

Promotion

The fourth element of marketing is promotion. Promotion may be the most important element of the marketing mix for many online programs, as the other three elements are largely predetermined and inflexible. With that in mind, it will be necessary to consider all the elements of the promotion mix when developing the integrated marketing communication plan. The institution should evaluate each communication option in the context of the intended target audience, the program's positioning, and any institutional constraints.

There are many ways of promoting the online program that are both effective and efficient. Which promotion methods should be used and how much should be spent on promotion is largely a matter of institutional choice. For many online education programs, promotion budgets are small. Selection of promotion mediums that are of little to no cost will likely take priority over more costly forms of promotion. Fortunately, many online education programs have shown much success, even utilizing modest promotion budgets.

The most utilized modes of promotion were reported by the Primary Research Group (2002) as some type of paid Internet advertising (85%), with over half of the responding institutions using newspaper and direct mail. There are six broad categories most often used for promoting online education. Five are listed below with brief commentary, the sixth, online marketing, has significantly more commentary.

Direct Marketing

The institution's own databases may offer a goldmine of potential students (i.e., alumni, students who dropped out, family of current students). Often, direct mail from the institution is already reaching these audiences. Placing flyers or small inserts regarding the online program along with existing mailings can be a cost-effective promotional method. In all cases, literature regarding the online programs should be distributed along with literature concerning traditional degree programs.

Traditional Advertising

Traditional print, radio, and television advertising have their roles in promoting the online education program. However, because of the cost involved, thorough research and planning should be conducted before making the decision to implement this method of promotion. Newspaper advertising was a prominent method for promotion of distance education programs, with more than half of all the programs advertised in newspapers and through direct mail (Primary Research Group, 2002).

Word of Mouth

Word of mouth has historically been one of the most effective methods of promotion. The fact that word-of-mouth promotion is largely free makes it even more attractive. The administration, faculty, staff, current students, and alumni are excellent conduits for passing along information regarding the online program, as long as they know about it and have a favorable opinion. Focused and clear internal communication to these audiences regarding the online program and its value is strategically important.

Public Relations/Publicity

The institutions public relations department is also a great resource for promoting the online program. News releases and other media targeted messages are acceptable and effective ways of promoting the online program. The institution's president, chancellor, and others dignitaries are often asked to speak and represent the institution at numerous functions and events each year. These engagements also provide an excellent opportunity to promote the online program. Clear and focused internal communications will be strategically important to the public relations/publicity marketing message.

Newsletter

Institutions often use newsletters (traditional print-based or electronic) to inform prospective students of upcoming events and/or the addition of new programs and courses. Electronic newsletters offer the opportunity for individuals to opt-in and opt-out, thereby creating a list of interested individuals that is accurate and targeted.

Online Marketing

Online marketing takes on a special significance for the online program. Because of the nature of the program and the pool of potential students available, this medium should be given special attention. As with the larger marketing message, the online campaign must also be clear, concise, and consistent. The institution should still coordinate online efforts in order to maximize the effectiveness of the online program's marketing.

Prospective online students routinely seek information about online programs by using the Internet. For most online programs, providing information about the program on the Internet is the single most effective method for reaching prospective students. Most "online" marketing campaigns are not aimed at creating a need as many potential students are already looking for an online program, but providing a message that meets a preexisting need. Therefore, online messages are designed to grab attention rather than to persuade.

Online marketing is also cost effective in relation to traditional media. Typically, "online conversion rates fall between six and eight percent" (Gallagher, 2003). Gallagher, an Eduventures analyst, suggests, "The average cost per lead online for distance education programs is $10 to $25, whereas offline media costs range from $50 to $2,000. Online promotion is categorized into several distinct promotional methods: institutional website, search engine optimization, hierarchically organized directories, pay-for-placement listings, distance education portals, keyword targeted advertising, banner advertisement, and email advertising.

Table 8.2.   Online Marketing Books

- *Integrated Marketing for Colleges, Universities and Schools: A Step-By-Step Planning Guide* by Robert A. Sevier (Editor)
- *Online Promotions: Winning Strategies and Tactics* by Bill Carmody
- *Planning Your Internet Marketing Strategy* by Ralph F. Wilson
- *Tactical Guide to Online Marketing* by Tig Tillinghast

Institutional Website.   Prospective students will seek out information regarding online education on the institution's website. The online program should be linked from the main home page, or at a minimum, be prominently displayed and linked on the academic information or degree program pages. Administrators should ensure that the institution's search engine software will return links to the online program if keywords are entered such as "online degree," "online degree program," "online graduate degree," "online program," "online classes," "Web-based class," "e-classes," "Internet classes," and so forth.

Search Engine Optimization.   Search engines (Google, Lycos, AOL, MSN, etc.) use algorithms to rank search results for display. Most individuals seldom go beyond the first page of results so optimizing the institution's pages to be displayed first is important. Search engine optimization attempts to decipher the salient features of search algorithms to achieve a higher ranking. The institution must promote the program using proper keywords in the Web pages to be successful. Institutions cannot depend completely on search engine optimization because success is sometimes sporadic. Nonetheless, search engine optimization is a low cost and effective method.

Hierarchically Organized Directories.   Hierarchically organized directories such as Yahoo and the Open Directory Project are often free for basic listings and allow the user to zero in on a specific program of interest.

Pay-for-Placement Listings.   Capitalizing on the demand for high search engine rankings, pay-for-placement options within search engines allows advertisers to bid for their position. Those who bid the most for a given keyword receive the highest ranking in the search results. Google uses a combination of price paid and search relevance to order the display of the ad. There are three popular aggregators for pay-for-placement listings: Google, Overture, and Ad Buyer (Lycos).

Distance Education Portals.   There are at many Web-based portals (www. onlineuc.net, www.petersons.com/distancelearning, www.ed-x.com, www. distancegradschools.com, www.degreeinfo.com, www.distancelearn.about. com, www.worldwidelearn.com, www.elearners.com, www.classesusa.com, and www.newsweekdistancelearning.com) that will list an institution's online program offering alongside other offerings from similar institutions. Payment for these services may be straight fee based or pay-per-lead.

Keyword Targeted Advertising.   Search engines allow advertisements to appear on keyword search pages, usually at the top or right of the search listing. This method is successfully used by the University of Phoenix and other institutions on Google, Yahoo, and others.

Banner Advertisement. Banners ads are a common form of online advertising; however, banner advertising is less effective and may carry a stigma of less-than-reputable advertising.

Email Advertising. The use of unsolicited email (spam) should be avoided at all cost. Opt-in e-mail lists, hoever, can be helpful for keeping potential students in touch with the institution. Including a way for potential students to opt-in via a "keep me informed" link provides excellent low-cost opportunities.

CHAPTER 9

CONCLUSION

A conclusion is the place where you got tired of thinking.

—Paul Dickson

Titling this chapter as the "Conclusion" is a bit deceptive; "Introduction" might be more descriptive. These final pages in no way seek to suggest that what is offered is the final verdict on successful practices for online education administration. Online education is rapidly evolving and changing; higher education is remarkably diverse; innovations and research are bringing much-needed insight into the way online students learn and what services and support are necessary for effectiveness. This chapter, however, pulls the strongest message from a chorus of voices into a somewhat harmonious crescendo.

Online education attracted much uncorroborated criticism as well as unsubstantiated hype. Through all the rhetoric and noise, online educa-tion pioneers persisted and insisted in seeking genuine results, and indeed, they have found them. The raw numbers of students and faculty involved in online education today speaks loudly but the qualitative data gathered from course evaluations and student interviews points to even greater potential. Achieving that potential is what online education administration should be focused on.

Online education administration takes patience, persistence, and per-spiration. Leading a new paradigm is not an easy task. Fortunately, the investigative and open nature of academe offers support. In addition to the current literature, Moore (as cited in Berge & Schrum, 1998) reminds

An Administrator's Guide to Online Education, 145–148

us that while online education is new, the practice of distance education is not. There is a substantial amount of distance education literature, theory, and previous practice that hold promise for the online educator.

Consistent themes are apparent throughout the literature and the widespread practices of the hundreds of institutions engaged in online education. Contrary to some early beliefs, online education requires substantial institutional involvement; students and faculty require increased support, both technically and pedagogically; policy must be both created and adapted; technology must be deployed in a stable and utilizable manner; the program must meet high academic expectations as well as find its identity in the marketplace; and, perhaps most importantly, if the program is to be sustained over time, it must find a place within the mainstream institution.

High levels of institutional commitment cannot be overlooked as a determining factor in online program success. The literature urges for a strong institutional leader to champion the online program and garner the support of the institution's organizations. A champion who can assist in gaining the faculty's acceptance of online education and who can seek ways to reward the faculty who participate is an invaluable asset. Strategic planning with key administrators that focus efforts upon specific and measurable goals while recognizing the needs of the population may offer the most value to the online program in terms of institutional commitment.

Program success is dependent upon student success and students need support to be successful. Since online education draws students from locations far removed from the campus, the institution must be vigilant in providing support to those students by nontraditional methods. Student support centered on providing the resources to achieve academic success with the least amount of distractions must be achieved not only because it's the right thing to do, but also because it is essential to remain viable in an increasingly competitively marketplace.

Program success is dependent upon faculty success; accordingly, faculty need support to be effective. The nuances of online course creation and instruction are not elements most faculty intrinsically understand. Successful programs created formal and informal support networks that not only train faculty but encourage and motivate them as well. Long-term program success appears linked to committed faculty participating in online education. That participation is closely linked to policy that recognizes both intrinsic and extrinsic motivations.

Existing institutional policy, unfortunately, is rarely supportive of online education without substantial modification and/or addition. Institutions are encouraged to take a policy analysis approach to ensure that the institutional frameworks fairly and equally provide for the needs of online students and faculty. Successful online education administrators create a supportive environment within the institution where online education is given the opportunity to succeed. A successful administrator has both a vision for the future with the stamina to plow through the daily requirements of introducing a new concept into an old infrastructure.

Program success is also tied to technology and therefore technical support cannot be ignored. Technology is expensive, unpredictable, and essential. While the present courseware management system marketplace is solid and competitive, new challenges offer even greater promise. Technology's importance is obvious, yet attaining the balance of adding innovative technologies while continuing to provide a strong and stable infrastructure is no small task. Online programs are finding ways to establish strategic relationships with IT departments that are often overwhelmed with competing institutional priorities.

There is ample indication that the honeymoon period for online education is coming to a close. Legislators, administrators, and faculty alike are asking hard questions and demanding real results from online education programs. Researchers are delivering strong evidence to the achievements, yet, they are also uncovering equally important reservations. Complacency cannot be accepted. While that often means hard choices must be made, administrators across the academy are achieving the change needed to continue the transformational growth of online education.

The continued growth of online education is bringing increased competition from nonprofits and for-profit institutions alike. Savvy marketing is not something higher education is necessarily known for; however, many nonprofit institutions, taking note of the marketing successes of for-profit institutions, are learning and adapting. Successful programs of the future will become proficient marketers in a highly competitive world.

Finally, and perhaps most importantly, online education needs to find a place within the mainstream of the institution. The call for mainstreaming online education is both valid and increasing in frequency. It is a common theme that permeates through dialogue at all levels. The need for an administrative champion, faculty buy-in, adequate support, and appropriate policy all have the common thread of the need to mainstream acceptance of online education in the institution's priorities and processes. Programs that are not directly linked to the institution's mission have little chance of succeeding over the long term. Gaining that institutional acceptance is the online administrator's greatest challenge but will also bring the most reward.

Online education administration is not an easy task, but it is an exceptionally rewarding endeavor. What online administrators have accomplished in this first decade is astounding. The lives of millions of individuals have been enriched. Institutions have received new life and increased revenues. Pedagogies have been advanced and faculty have renewed their interest in instructional design and instructional methodologies.

This book can indeed only be the introduction to a revolution that shows almost infinite promise. Higher education has only begun to understand the most basic of fundamentals that drive online program success. Those fundamentals will become the cornerstones of a much brighter future. We can only look with anticipation as the next decade in online education promises to be both as exciting and groundbreaking as the first. It is truly an exciting time to be an educator.

REFERENCES

Adams, J. C., & Seagren, A. T. (2004). Distance education strategy: Mental models and strategic choices. *Online Journal of Distance Learning Administration, 7*(2) [Online serial]. Available from http://www.westga.edu/~distance/ojdla/summer72/adams72.html

Adkins, M. (2004). *New service connects prospective online faculty with institutions offering online courses* [Press release]. Montgomery, AL: Faculty Finder. Retrieved January 21, 2005, from https://www.facultyfinder.com/index.cfm?fa=corp.newsDetails&newsID=4

Allen, I. E., & Seaman, J. (2003). *Sizing the opportunity: The quality and extent of online education in the United States, 2002 and 2003*. Needham, MA: Sloan Consortium.

Allen, I. E., & Seaman, J. (2004). *Entering the mainstream: The quality and extent of online education in the United States, 2003 and 2004*. Needham, MA: Sloan Consortium.

American Association of University Professors. (1999). *Statement on distance education*. Washington, DC: Author. Available from http://www.aaup.org/statements/Redbook/StDistEd.HTM

American Council on Education. (2000, March). *Developing a distance education policy for 21st century learning*. Washington, DC: Author.

Ananthanarayanan, V. (2000). *Online support services for distance education: Proposed information dissemination and communication flow infrastructure*. Unpublished master's thesis, Abilene Christian University, Abilene, TX.

Arabasz, P., Boggs, R., & Baker, M. B. (2003, April 29). Highlights of e-learning support practices. *EDUCAUSE Center for Applied Research Research Bulletin, 2003*(9), 1–11. Retrieved March 22, 2005, from http://www.educause.edu/ir/library/pdf/ERB0309.pdf

Arnone, M. (2001, November 16). 3 companies that sell course software say they are raking in money. *Chronicle of Higher Education, 48*(12), A40.

Bart, C. (1998). Mission matters. *CPA Journal, 68*(8), 56–57.

Bates, A. W. (2000). *Managing technological change: Strategies for college and university leaders*. San Francisco: Jossey-Bass.

Baus, F., & Ramsbottom, C. (1999). Starting and sustaining a consortium. In L. Dotolo & J. Strandness (Eds.), *Best practices in higher education consortia: How institutions can work together* (No. 106, pp. 3–18). San Francisco: Jossey-Bass.

Beard, L. A., Harper, C., & Riley, G. (2004). Online versus on-campus instruction: Student attitudes & perceptions. *Techtrends, 48*(6), 29–31.

Beaudoin, M. (2003). Distance education leadership: An appraisal of research and practice. In M. G. Moore & W. G. Anderson (Eds.), *Handbook of distance education* (pp. 519–530). Mahwah, NJ: Erlbaum.

Berg, G. A. (2002). *Why distance learning?: Higher education administrative practices*. Westport, CT: Oryx Press.

Berge, Z. L. (1998). Barriers to online teaching in post-secondary institutions: Can policy changes fix it? *Online Journal of Distance Learning Administration, 1*(2) [Online serial]. Available from http://www.westga.edu/~distance/Berge12.html

Berge, Z. L. (Ed.). (2001). *Sustaining distance training*. San Francisco: Jossey-Bass.

Berge, Z. L., & Muilenburg, L. Y. (2000). Barriers to distance education as perceived by managers and administrators: Results of a survey. In M. Clay (Ed.), *Distance Learning Administration Annual 2000*. Carrollton, GA: Online Journal of Distance Learning Administration. Available from http://userpages.umbc.edu/~berge/gl/man_admin.html

Berge, Z. L., & Schrum, L. (1998). Linking strategic planning with program implementation for distance education. *Cause/Effect, 21*(3), 31–38.

Berra, Y., & Kaplan, D. (2001). *When you come to a fork in the road, take it!: Inspiration and wisdom from one of baseball's greatest heroes*. New York: Hyperion.

Best of the online grad programs. (2001, October 15). *U. S. News and World Report, 131*(15), 62–63.

Betts, K. S. (1998). An institutional overview: Factors influencing faculty participation in distance education in postsecondary education in the United States: An institutional study. *Online Journal of Distance Learning Administration, 1*(3) [Online serial]. Available from http://www.westga.edu/~distance/betts13.html

Birnbaum, W. S. (2004). *Strategic thinking: A four piece puzzle*. Costa Mesa, CA: Douglas Mountain.

Blaisdell, M. (2005, January). It's the support, stupid! *Campus Technology, 18*(5), 36–39.

Boettcher, J. V. (2004a, November). Are we there yet? *Campus Technology, 18*(3), 22–23, 26.

Boettcher, J. V. (2004b). Design levels for distance and online learning. In C. Howard, K. Schenk, & R. Discenza (Eds.), *Distance learning and university effectiveness: Changing educational paradigms for online learning* (pp. 21–54). Hershey, PA: Information Science.

Bower, B. L. (2001). Distance education: Facing the faculty challenge. *Online Journal of Distance Learning Administration, 4*(2) [Online serial]. Available from http://www.westga.edu/~distance/ojdla/summer42/bower42.html

Bozarth, J., Chapman, D. D., & LaMonica, L. (2004). Preparing for distance learning: Designing an online student orientation. *Educational Technology & Society, 7*(1), 87–106.

Brezil, C. (2000). Lessons for higher education from the dot coms. *EDUCAUSE Quarterly, 23*(4), 47–49.

Buchanan, E. A. (1999). Assessment measures: Pre-test for successful distance teaching and learning? *Online Journal of Distance Learning Administration, 2*(3) [Online serial]. Available from http://www.westga.edu/~distance/buchanan24.html

Buchanan, E. A. (2000). Going the extra mile: Serving distance education students. *Online Journal of Distance Learning Administration, 3*(1) [Online serial]. Available from http://www.westga.edu/~distance/buchanan31.html

Buchanan, E. A. (2002). Institutional and library services for distance education courses and programs. In R. Discenza, C. Howard, & K. Schenk (Eds.), *The design & management of effective distance learning programs* (pp. 141–154). Hershey, PA: Idea Group.

Cain, D. L., & Lockee, B. (2002). *Student support services at a distance: are institutions meeting the needs of distance learners?* (ERIC Document Reproduction Service No. ED468729)

Cain, D. L., Marrara, C., Pitre, P. E., & Armour, S. (2003). Support services that matter: An exploration of the experiences and needs of graduate students in a distance learning environment. *Journal of Distance Education, 18*(1), 42–56.

Care, W. D., & Scanlan, J. M. (2001). Planning and managing the development of courses for distance delivery: Results from a qualitative study. *Online Journal of Distance Learning Administration, 4*(2) [Online serial]. Available from http://www.westga.edu/~distance/ojdla/summer42/care42.html

Carnevale, D. (2004a, April 30). For online adjuncts, a seller's market. *Chronicle of Higher Education, 50*(34), A31.

Carnevale, D. (2004b, July 30). Many online courses work best at no distance at all. *Chronicle of Higher Education, 50*(47), A22.

Carnevale, D. (2004c, March 5). Western Washington U. will eschew protection of new copyright law. *Chronicle of Higher Education, 50*(26), A28.

Carnevale, D. (2004d, March 26). Whether online or in a classroom, courses take about the same amount of time to teach, study finds. *Chronicle of Higher Education, 50*(29), A31.

Carnevale, D., & Olsen, F. (2003, June 13). How to succeed in distance education. *Chronicle of Higher Education, 49*(40), A31.

Carr, S. (2001, February 16). Is anyone making money on distance education? *Chronicle of Higher Education, 47*(23), A41.

Cavanaugh, C. (2002a). Distance education quality: The resources–practices–results cycle and the standards. In *World Conference on E-Learning in Corporate., Government., Health, & Higher Education 2002*(1), 168–173.

Cavanaugh, C. (2002b). Distance education quality: Success factors for resources, practices, and results. In R. Discenza, C. Howard, & K. Schenk (Eds.), *The design and management of effective distance learning programs* (pp. 171–189). Hershey, PA: Idea Group.

Charp, S. (2000, April). Distance education. *T.H.E. Journal, 27*(9), 10–12.

College media group cautions that 2 copyright laws could collide. (2003, March 28). *Chronicle of Higher Education, 49*(29), A29.

The Commission on Colleges: Southern Association of Colleges, and Schools. (1997). *Distance education policy statement*. Decatur, Georgia: Author. Retrieved August 1, 2004, from http://www.sacscoc.org/pdf/distance.pdf

Compora, D. (2003). Current trends in distance education: An administrative model. *Online Journal of Distance Learning Administration, 6*(2) [Online serial]. Available from http://www.westga.edu/~distance/ojdla/summer62/compora62.html

Computer History Museum. (2004). *Internet history*. Retrieved June 3, 2004, from http://www.computerhistory.org/exhibits/internet_history/internet_history_90s.shtml

The Connecticut Distance Learning Consortium, (2003). *CTDLC: Mission statement*. Retrieved June 30, 2004, from http://ctdlc.org./About/mission.html

Council for Adult and Experiential Learning (CAEL). (2003). *CAEL industry-led online learning: Factors contributing to high completion rates in industry-led online courses*. Chicago: Author.

The Declaration of Independence. (1776). Retrieved August 9, 2004, from The National Archives Experience Web site: http://www.archives.gov/national_archives_ experience/charters/declaration.html

Dede, C. (1993). Leadership without followers. In G. Kearsley & W. Lynch (Eds.), *Educational technology: Leadership perspectives* (pp. 19-28). Englewood Cliffs, NJ: Educational Technology Publications.

Dillon, C. L., & Cintrón, R. (Eds.). (1997). Distance education and the community college: From convention to vision. In C. L. Dillon & R. Cintrón (Eds.) *Building a working policy for distance education* (pp. 93-100). San Francisco: Jossey-Bass.

Dolak, F. (2001, December). The ghosts of copyright: Past, preset, and future. *Instructional Telecommunications Council News*.

Dooley, K. E., & Magill, J. (2002). Faculty perceptions and participation in distance education: Pick fruit from the low-hanging branches. In R. Discenza, C. Howard, & K. Schenk (Eds.), *The design & management of effective distance learning programs* (pp. 75-92). Hershey, PA: Idea Group.

Dunn, S. (2000). The virtualizing of education. *Futurist, 34*(2), 34.

Dupin-Bryant, P. A. (2004). Pre-entry variable related to retention in online distance education. *The American Journal of Distance Education, 18*(4), 199-206.

Easley, H. (2002, August 12). Mixed success for online colleges [Electronic version]. *The Journal News*. Retrieved June 3, 2004, from The Journal News Web site: http://www.thejournalnews.com/newsroom/081202/12online.html

Edmonds, C. D. (2003). *Providing access to students with disabilities in online distance education: Legal, technical, and practical considerations*. Paper presented at the 10th annual International Distance Education Conference, Austin, TX. Retrieved December 30, 2004, from http://www.cdlr.tamu.edu/dec_2003/decProceedings/7-Edmunds-Providing%20Access%20to%20Students%20with%20Disabilities1.pdf

Edmonds, C. D. (2004). Providing access in online distance education: Legal and technical concerns for higher education. *American Journal of Distance Education, 18*(1), 51–62.

Edmonds, G. (1999, March). Making change happen: Planning for success. *The Technology Source*. Retrieved June 3, 2004, from http://ts.mivu.org/default. asp?show=article&id=40.

Eduventures. (2002, September). *Distance learning at the tipping point: Critical success factors to grow fully online distance education programs*. Boston: Gallagher & Newman.

eCollege.com. (1999). *How to successfully market your campus*. Denver, CO: Author.

Evans, T. (2003). Policy and planning in the developed countries: Coping with compulsive development cultures. In S. Panda (Ed.), *Planning and management in distance education* (pp. 31–39). London: Kogan Page.

Finkelstein, M., & Scholz, B. (2000). What do we know about information technology and the cost of collegiate teaching and learning. In M. J. Finklestein, C. Frances, & F. Jewett (Eds.), *Dollars, distance, and online education: The new economics of college teaching and learning* (pp. 3–34). Phoenix, AZ: Oryx Press.

Fuchs, I. (2004, September 24). Needed: An "educore" to aid collaboration. *Chronicle of Higher Education, 51*(5), B19.

Fulkerth, R. (1999). Keys to the culture: Factors in successful dl implementation. In *Proceedings of World Conference on Educational Multimedia, Hypermedia and Telecommunications (EDMEDIA)* (Vol. 1, pp. 658–662). Norfolk, VA: AACE. Available from http://dl.aace.org/4322

Gaide, S. (2004). Using policy to "mainstream" distance ed programs. *Distance Education Report, 8*(6), 1, 4.

Gallagher, S. (2003). A brave new world: Trends, strategies & best practices in internet marketing for distance education. In *2003 Fall Distance Education Workshop*. Tucson, AZ: Distance Education and Training Council.

Garrison, R. (2000). Theoretical challenges for distance education in the 21st century: A shift from structural to transactional issues. *International Review of Research in Open and Distance Learning, 1*(1), 1–17.

Garrison, D. R., & Anderson, T. (2003). *E-Learning in the 21st century: A framework for research and practice*. London: Routledge.

Gellman-Danley, B., & Fetzner, M. J. (1998). Asking the really tough questions: Policy issues for distance learning. *Online Journal of Distance Learning Administration, 1*(1) [Online serial]. Available from http://www.westga.edu/~distance/danley11.html

Gibbons, H., & Wentworth, G. (2002). Processes for motivating online learners from recruitment through degree completion. *Virtual University Gazette: Motivating and Retaining Adult Learners Online, August*, 127–135.

Green, K. C. (2001). *Campus computing, 2001: The 12th national survey of computing and information technology in American higher education*. Resources in Education and ERIC Document Reproduction Service No. ED459679

Guidelines for Distance Learning Library Services. (2004). Retrieved December 30, 2004, from http://www.ala.org/ala/acrl/acrlstandards/guidelinesdistance learning.htm

Gunawardena, C., & McIsaac, M. (2003). Distance education. In D. H. Jonassen (Ed.), *Handbook of research in educational communications and technology* (2nd ed., pp. 355–395). Mahwah, NJ: Erlbaum.

Haché, D. (Summer 1998). Strategic planning of distance education in the age of teleinformatics. *Online Journal of Distance Learning Administration, 1*(2) [Online serial]. Available from http://www.westga.edu/~distance/Hache12.html

Hafner, K. (2002, May 2). Lessons learned at dot-com u. *New York Times*, p. G1.

Hanna, D. (2003). Organizational models in higher education, past and future. In M. G. Moore & W. G. Anderson (Eds.), *Handbook of distance education* (pp. 67–78). Mahwah, NJ: Erlbaum.

Hartman, J., Dziuban, D., & Moskal, P. (2000). Faculty satisfaction in ALNs: A dependent or independent variable. In J. Bourne (Ed.), *On-line education: Learning effectiveness and faculty satisfaction* (pp. 154–179). Nashville, TN: Vanderbilt University Center for Asynchronous Learning Networks. Retrieved May 14, 2002, from http://www.sloan-c.org/publications/jaln/v4n3/pdf/v4n3_hartman.pdf

Haughey, M. (2003). Planning for open and flexible learning. In S. Panda (Ed.), *Planning & management in distance education* (pp. 53-62). London: Kogan Page.

Hawkins, B. L. (1999). Distributed learning and institutional restructuring. *Educom Review, 34*(4), 12–15.

Hawkins, B. L., Rudy, J. A., & Madsen, J. W. (2003). *EDUCAUSE core data service 2002 summary report* (PUB8000). Boulder, CO: EDUCAUSE.

Hawksley, R., & Owen, J. (2002). *Going the distance: Are there common factors in high performing distance learning?* London: Learning and Skills Development Agency.

Heerema, D. L., & Rogers, R. L. (2001, December). Avoiding the quality/quantity trade-off in distance education. *The Journal, 29*(5), 14–21. Available from http://www.thejournal.com/magazine/vault/articleprintversion.cfm?aid=3753

Hitch, L. P., & MacBrayne, P. (2003, March/April). A model for effectively supporting e-learning. *The Technology Source*. Retrieved March 22, 2005, from http://ts.mivu.org/default.asp?show=article&id=1016

Howard, C., Schenk, K., & Discenza, R. (2004). *Distance learning and university effectiveness: Changing educational paradigms for online learning*. Hershey, PA: Information Science.

Howell, S. L., Williams, P. B., & Lindsay, N. K. (2003). Thirty-two trends affecting distance education: An informed foundation for strategic planning. *Online Journal of Distance Learning Administration, 6*(3) [Online serial]. Available from http://www.westga.edu/~distance/ojdla/fall63/howell63.html

Husson, W. J., & Waterman, E. K. (2002). Quality measures in distance learning [Electronic version]. *Higher Education in Europe, 27*(3), 253–260.

Implementing ADL. (2003). Retrieved March 29, 2005, from http://www.adlnet.org/index.cfm?fuseaction=abtadl

IMS Global Learning Consortium. (n.d.). Retrieved January 5, 2005, from http://www.imsglobal.org

The Institute for Higher Education Policy. (1998, May). *Student aid for distance learners: Charting a new course* (Summary and Proceedings of The Roundtable on Student Aid for Distance Learners). Washington, DC: The Institute for Higher Education Policy.

Johnson, J. (2003). *Distance education: The complete guide to design, delivery, and improvement*. New York: Teachers College Press.

Johnstone, S. (2002, August). When online services reflect bad policies. *Syllabus, 16*(1). Retrieved November 11, 2002, from http://www.syllabus.com/article.asp?id=6591

Katz, R. (2001, Fall). Changing practices and new frontiers. In G. R. Maughan (Series Ed.) & M. Kramer (Vol. Ed.), *New directions for higher education: Number 115* (No. 115, pp. 95–105). San Francisco: Jossey-Bass.

Keegan, D. (1983). *Six distance education theorists*. Hagen: Fernuniversität (ZIFF).

Keegan, D. (1996). *Foundations of distance education* (3rd ed.). London: Routledge Press.

Kennedy, J. F. (Speaker). (1961). *Special message to the Congress on urgent national needs* [Audio file]. Boston: John F. Kennedy Library and Museum. Retrieved May 22, 2004, from http://www.cs.umb.edu/~rwhealan/jfk/j052561.htm

Kinash, S., Crichton, S., & Kim-Rupnow, W. S. (2004). A review of 2000-2003 literature at the intersection of online learning and disability. *American Journal of Distance Education, 18*(1), 5–19.

King, J. W., Lacy, D., McMillian, J., Bartels, K., & Freddolino, M. (1998, September). *The policy perspective in distance education: A futures landscape/panorama*. Paper presented at the Nebraska Distance Education Conference, Lincoln, NE.

King, J., Nugent, G. C, Eich, J., Mlinek, D., & Russell, E. (2000). Policy framework for distance education: A case study and model. *DEOSNEWS, 10*(10). Available from http://www.ed.psu.edu/acsde/deos/deosnews/deosnews10_10.asp

King, J. W., Nugent, G. C., Russell, E. B., Eich, J., & Lacy, D. D. (2000). Policy frameworks for distance education: Implications for decision makers. *Online Journal of Distance Learning Administration, 3*(2) [Online serial]. Available from http://www.westga.edu/~distance/king32.html

Kofahi, N. A., & Srinivas, N. (2004). Distance learning: Major issues and challenges. *International Journal of Instructional Technology & Distance Learning, 1*(5). [Online serial]. Available from http://www.itdl.org/Journal/May_04/article02.htm

Kovel-Jarboe, P. (1997). From the margin to the mainstream: State-level policy and planning for distance education. In C. L. Dillon & R. Cintrón (Eds.), *Building a working policy for distance education* (No. 99, pp. 23–32). San Francisco: Jossey-Bass.

Kretovics, M. (2003). The role of student affairs in distance education: Cyber-services or virtual communities. *Online Journal of Distance Learning Administration, 6*(3) [Online serial]. Available from http://www.westga.edu/~distance/ojdla/fall63/kretovics63.html

Lane-Maher, M., & Ashar, H. (2001). Students.edu: Guidelines for online education programs. *EDUCAUSE Quarterly, 24*(1), 26–31.

LaPadula, M. (2003). A comprehensive look at online student support services for distance learners. *The American Journal of Distance Education, 17*(2), 119–128.

Lape, D. H., & Hart, P. K. (1997). Changing the way we teach by changing the college: Leading the way together. In C. L. Dillon & R. Cintrón (Eds.), *Building a working policy for distance education* (No. 99, pp. 15–22). San Francisco: Jossey Bass.

Lee, J. (2001). Instructional support for distance education and faculty motivation, commitment, satisfaction. *British Journal of Educational Technology, 32*(2), 153–160.

Levin, H. M., & McEwan, P. J. (2000). *Cost-effectiveness analysis: Methods and applications* (2nd ed.). Thousand Oaks, CA: Sage.

Levine, A., & Sun, J. C. (2002). Barriers to distance education. *American Council on Education Center for Policy Analysis* (No. 309379). Available from http://www.acenet.edu/bookstore/pdf/distributed-learning/distributed-learning-06.pdf

Levy, Y., & Ramim, M. (2004). Financing expensive technologies in an era of decreased funding. In C. Howard, K. Schenk, & R. Discenza (Eds.), *Distance learning and university effectiveness: Changing educational paradigms for online learning* (pp. 278–301). Hershey, PA: Information Science.

Lorenzo, G. (2002). Marketing distance education. *Educational Pathways*. Retrieved May 30, 2004, from http://www.edpath.com/marketing.htm

Lynch, M. M. (2001, November/December). Effective student preparation for online learning. *The Technology Source*, p. 6.

MacKay, C. (1841). *Extraordinary popular delusions and the madness of crowds.* London: Richard Bentley.

Maddux, C. D. (2003). Fads, distance education, and the importance of theory. In M. Corry & C. Tu (Eds.), *Distance education: What works well* (pp. 121–127). New York: Haworth Press.

Maddux, C. D., Ewing-Taylor, J., & Johnson, D. L. (2002). The light and dark sides of distance education. In C. D. Maddux, J. Ewing-Taylor, & D. L. Johnson (Eds.), *Distance education: Issues and concerns* (pp. 1–7). New York: Haworth Press.

Marcus, S. (2004). Leadership in distance education: Is it a unique type of leadership—A literature review. *Online Journal of Distance Learning Administration, 7*(1) [Online serial]. Available from http://www.westga.edu/~distance/ojdla/spring71/marcus71.html

Market Data Retrieval. (2005). *The college technology review* (2004–2005 academic year). Shelton, CT: Author.

Martz Jr., W. B., Reddy, V. K., & Sangermano, K. (2004). Looking for indicators of success for distance education. In C. Howard, K. Schenk, & R. Discenza (Eds.), *Distance learning and university effectiveness: Changing educational paradigms for online learning* (pp. 144–160). Hershey, PA: Idea Group.

Matthews, D. (1999, September). The origins of distance education and its use in the United States. *T.H.E. Journal, 27*(2), 54–67.

Matthews, D. A. (2002). Distance education: What is it? In R. Discenza, C. Howard, & K. Schenk (Eds.), *The design and management of effective distance learning programs* (pp. 1–20). Hershey, PA: Idea Group.

McCarthy, J. E. (1960). *Basic marketing: A managerial approach.* Homewood, IL: Irwin.

McCloskey, P. (2002, September). Syllabus2002 conference review: Innovations battle budgets for elearning market share. *Syllabus, 16*(2), 18–22. Retrieved April 3, 2003, from http://www.campus-technology.com/print.asp?ID=6703

McCune, S. D. (1986). *Guide to strategic planning for educators.* Alexandria, VA: Association for Supervision and Curriculum Development.

McGorry, S. Y. (2003). Measuring quality in online programs. *The Internet and Higher Education, 6,* 159–177.

McNamara, C. (1999). *Basics of developing mission, vision, and values statements.* Retrieved September 4, 2004, from http://www.mapnp.org/library/plan_dec/str_plan/stmnts.htm#anchor522740

McNeil, J. M. (1997) *Americans with disabilities: 1994–95* (Current Population Reports: Series P70-61). Washington, DC: US Department of Commerce, Economics and Statistics Administration, Bureau of the Census. Available from http://www.census.gov/prod/3/97pubs/p70-61.pdf

McPherson, M. A. & Baptista Nunes, J. M. (2004, March 4-6). The role of tutors in the delivery of e-learning. In *Proceedings of the 3rd Research Workshop of the European Distance Education Network (EDEN) on Research and Policy in open and distance learning* (pp. 317-323). Oldenburg, Germany: European Distance Education Network.

McVay, M. (2000). *Developing a web-based distance student orientation to enhance student success in an online bachelor's degree completion program.* Doctoral dissertation, Nova Southeastern University. Available from http://web.pdx.edu/~mmlynch/McVay-dissertation.pdf

Menager-Beeley, R. (2001, October). *Student success in web based distance learning: Measuring motivation to identify at risk students and improve retention in online classes.* Paper presented at the Webnet 2001: World Conference on the WWW and Internet Proceeding, Orlando, FL.

Meyer, K. (2002). *Quality in distance education: Focus on on-line learning* (Vol. 29). San Francisco: Jossey-Bass.

Milheim, W. (2001). Faculty and administrative strategies for the effective implementation of distance education. *British Journal of Educational Technology, 32*(5), 535–542.

Miller, T. W., & King, F. B. (2003). Distance education: Pedagogy and best practices in the new millennium. *International Journal of Leadership in Education, 6*(3), 283–297.

Mintzberg, H. (1994). *The rise and fall of strategic planning.* New York: Free Press.

Mintzberg, H., Quinn, J., & Voyer, J. (1995). *The strategy process: Collegiate edition.* Englewood Cliffs, NJ: Prentice Hall.

Moore, K., Bartkovich, J., Fetzner, M., & Ison, S. (2002, June). *Success in cyberspace: Student retention in online courses.* Paper presented at the Annual Forum for the Association for Institutional Research, Toronto, ON, Canada.

Moore, M. G. (1993). Is teaching like flying? A total systems view of distance education. *American Journal of Distance Education, 7*(1), 1–10.

Moore, M. G. (2003). Editorial: Learner support. *American Journal of Distance Education, 17*(3), 141–143.

Moore, M. G., & Kearsley, G. (1996). *Distance education: A systems view.* Belmont, CA: Wadsworth.

Moore, M., & Kearsley, G. (2005). *Distance education: A systems view* (2nd ed.). Belmont, CA: Wadsworth.

National Education Association. (2000, June). *A survey of traditional and distance learning higher education members.* Washington, DC: Abacus Associates.

Nielsen, J. (2000). *Designing web usability: The practice of simplicity.* Indianapolis, IN: New Riders.

Noonan, S. J. (2003). *The elements of leadership.* Lanhan, MD: Scarecrow Education.

Northern Arizona University (n.d.). *Traits for successful online learners.* Retrieved July 24, 2005, from Preparing for WebCT Web site: http://www2.nau.edu/ctel/preparing/success/traits.htm

Oblinger, D., & Kidwell, J. (2002, May/June). Distance learning: Are we being realistic? *EDUCAUSE Review, 35,* 30–39.

O'Brien, B. S., & Renner, A. L. (2002). Online student retention: Can it be done? *World Conference on Educational Multimedia, Hypermedia and Telecommunications 2002, 1,* 1479–1483.

Olsen, F. (2002, November 1). Phoenix rises. *Chronicle of Higher Education, 49*(10), A29.

Olson, M. (2004, June). What price profit? *NACUBO Business Officer, 37*(12), 18–21.

O'Quinn, L., & Corry, M. (2002). Factors that deter faculty from participating in distance education. *Online Journal of Distance Learning Administration, 5*(4) [Online serial]. Available from http://www.westga.edu/~distance/ojdla/winter54/Quinn54.htm

Pacey, L., & Keough, E. (2003). Public policy, institutional structures, and strategic implementation. In M. G. Moore & W. G. Anderson (Eds.), *Handbook of distance education* (pp. 401–416). Mahwah, NJ: Erlbaum.

Pankowski, P. (2004, Spring). Faculty training for online teaching [Electronic version]. *T.H.E. Journal.* Available from http://www.thejournal.com/magazine/vault/A5010.cfm

Parisot, A. (1997). Distance education as a catalyst for changing teaching in the community college: Implications for institutional policy. In C. L. Dillon & R. Cintrón (Eds.), *Building a working policy for distance education* (No. 99, pp. 5–13). San Francisco: Jossey-Bass.

Parker, A. (2003). Motivation and incentives for distance faculty. *Online Journal of Distance Learning Administration, 6*(3) [Online serial]. Available from http://www.westga.edu/~distance/ojdla/fall63/parker63.htm

The Penn State Distance Education Online Committee. (1996, August 1). *Distance education at Penn State: Vision, principles, and policies.* University Park, PA: Distance Education Online Committee. Available from http://www.outreach.psu.edu/de/programmatic_vision.html

Perraton, H. (2000). *Open and distance learning in the developing world.* London: Routledge Press.

Poley, J. K., & France, E. (1998, October). *Philosophy and purposes of distance education.* Paper presented at the American Distance Education Consortium, Lincoln, NE. Available from http://www.adec.edu/workshops/1998/sept28/paper.html

Pond, W. K. (2002). Distributed education in the 21st century: Implications for quality assurance. *Online Journal of Distance Learning Administration, 5*(2) [Online serial]. Available from http://www.westga.edu/~distance/ojdla/summer52/pond52.html

Porter, L. (1997). *Creating the virtual classroom: Distance learning on the Internet.* New York: Wiley Computer.

Prestera, G. E., & Moller, L. A. (2001). Organizational alignment supporting distance education in post-secondary institutions. *Online Journal of Distance Learning Administration, 4*(4) [Online serial]. Available from http://westga.edu/~distance/ojdla/winter44/presteraa44.html

Primary Research Group. (2002). *The survey of distance and cyberlearning programs in higher education, 2002–2003 edition.* New York: Primary Research Group Staff.

Rheingold, H. (2001, July 1). Face-to-face with virtual communities. *Syllabus, 15*(12), 8-12.

Robinson, E. T. (2004). Return on investment for distance education offerings. In C. Howard, K. Schenk, & R. Discenza (Eds.), *Distance learning and university effectiveness: Changing educational paradigms for online learning* (pp. 253–277). Hershey, PA: Information Science.

Robinson, J. (2005, January). OSS myths debunked! *Campus Technology, 18*(5), 52.

Rockwell, S. K., Shauer, J., Fritz, S. M., & Marx, D. B. (1999, Winter). Incentives and obstacles influencing higher education faculty and administrator to teach via distance. *Online Journal of Distance Learning Administration, 2*(3) [Online serial]. Available from http://www.westga.edu/~distance/rockwell24.html

Rumble, G. (2001). Re-inventing distance education, 1971–2001. *International Journal of Lifelong Education, 20*(1/2), 31–43.

Russell, C. (2002, November). Major copyright bill affecting distance education becomes law. *American Library Association Washington Office Newsline, 11*(87). Retrieved January 4, 2003, from http://www.ala.org/ala/washoff/washnews/20026/87nov04.htm

Saba, F. (September 19, 2004). Exclusive interview with Dr. Darcy W. Hardy, Assistant Vice Chancellor and Director, UT TeleCampus, The University Of Texas System. *Distance-Educator.* Retrieved January 21, 2005, from http://www.distance-educator.com/dnews/modules.php?op=modload&name=News&file=article&sid=11986

Sachs, S. G. (1999). The mature distance education program. *Performance Improvement Quarterly, 12*(2), 66–83.

Santovec, M. L. (2004, November 15). Strategies to ensure quality. *Distance Education Report, 8*(22), 1, 3, 7.

Saunders, G. (2002). The future of distance learning in the traditional university. In R. Discenza, C. Howard, & K. Schenk (Eds.), *The design & management of effective distance learning programs* (pp. 55–73). Hershey, PA: Idea Group.

Sausner, R. (2003, July). Carving your slice of the virtual pie. *University Business, 6*(7). Available from http://www.universitybusiness.com/page.cfm?p=311

Schifter, C. C. (2000). Compensation models in distance education: National survey questionnaire revisited. *Online Journal of Distance Learning Administration, 7*(1) [Online serial]. Available from http://www.westga.edu/~distance/schifter31.html

Schrum, L., & Benson, A. (2002). Establishing successful online distance learning environments: Distinguishing factors that contribute to online courses and programs. In R. Discenza, C. Howard, & K. Schenk (Eds.), *The design & management of effective distance learning programs* (pp. 190–204). Hershey, PA: Idea Group Publishing.

SCORM 1.2. (2003). Retrieved March 29, 2005, from http://www.adlnet.org/index.cfm?fuseaction=scorm12

SCORM 1.2 business rules and best practices. (2004). Retrieved March 29, 2005, from http://www.atsc.army.mil/itsd/imi/bus_rules.asp

Section 508, 1998 Amendment to the Rehabilitation Act (1973). (2005). Retrieved January 5, 2005, from http://www.umuc.edu/ade/li/sec508.html

Seehusen, V. (2000). A consortial approach to distance education delivery and management. *Community College Journal of Research and Practice, 24,* 27–36.

Sevier, R. A. (2002, May). The power of internal marketing. *University Business, 5*(5), 27.

Shelton, K. (2004, February). *Online education: Rooted in values for a new vision.* Plenary speech presented at the ACCESS/AABC Conference, Orlando, FL.

Shelton, K., & Saltsman, G. (2004). The dotcom bust: A postmortem lesson for online education. *Distance Learning, 1*(1), 19–27.

Simonson, M. (2002). Policy and distance education. *Quarterly Review of Distance Education, 3*(2), v–vii.

Simonson, M., & Bauck, T. (2003). Distance education policy issues: Statewide perspectives. In M. G. Moore & William G. Anderson (Eds.), *Handbook of distance education* (pp. 417–424). Mahwah, NJ: Erlbaum.

Simonson, M., Smaldino, S., Albright, M., & Zvacek, S. (2003). *Teaching and learning at a distance* (2nd ed.). Upper Saddle River, NJ: Merrill Prentice Hall.

Simpson, O. (2003). *Student retention in online, open and distance learning.* London: Kogan Page.

Smith, D. K. (1999). *Make success measurable.* New York: Wiley.

SREB Distance Learning Policy Laboratory Finance Subcommittee. (2002, August). Using finance policy to reduce barriers to distance learning. In *Series on distance learning policy issues.* Atlanta, GA: Distance Learning Policy Laboratory.

SREB Distance Learning Policy Laboratory Student Services Subcommittee. (2002, June). Anytime, anyplace services for the 21st century student. In *Series on distance learning policy issues.* Atlanta, GA: Distance Learning Policy Laboratory.

Stanford University. (1963). *A call to conscience: The landmark speeches of Dr. Martin Luther King, Jr.* Available from http://www.stanford.edu/group/King/publications/speeches/address_at_march_on_washington.pdf

Sumler, D. E. (2004, January). Unbundling the campus. *University Business, 7*(1), 7–8.

Sumner, J. (2000). Serving the system: A critical history of distance education. *Open Learning, 15*(3), 267–285.

Taylor, T. H., Parker III, G. D., & Tebeaux, E. (2001). Confronting cost and pricing issues in distance education. *EDUCAUSE Quarterly, 24*(3), 16–23.

TEACH act update. (2005, January). *Distance Education Report, 9*(1), 1–2, 6.

Thompson, M. D. (2004). Faculty self-study research project: Examining the online workload. *Journal of Asynchronous Learning Networks, 8*(3).

Tomei, L. (2004). The impact of online teaching on faculty load. *International Journal of Instructional Technology and Distance Learning, 1*(1) [Online serial]. Available from http://www.itdl.org/journal/Jan_04/article04.htm

Turoff, M., Discenza, R., & Howard, C. (2004). How distance programs will affect students, courses, faculty, and institutional futures. In C. Howard, K. Schenk, & R. Discenza (Eds.), *Distance learning and university effectiveness: Changing educational paradigms for online learning* (pp. pp. 1–20). Hershey, PA: Information Science.

U.S. Department of Education, National Center for Education Statistics. (2003). *Distance education at degree-granting postsecondary institutions: 2000–2001* (NCES 2003-017). Washington, DC: Author.

U.S. Department of Labor: Bureau of Labor Statistics. (1999, March). *Issues in labor statistics* (Summary 99-4). Washington, DC: U.S. Government Printing Office.

Verduin Jr., J. R., & Clark, T. A. (1991). *Distance education: The foundations of effective practice.* San Francisco: Jossey-Bass.

Watkins, B. L. (1991). A quite radical idea: the invention and elaboration of collegiate correspondence study. In B. L. Watkins & S. J. Wright (Eds.), *The foundations of American distance education: A century of collegiate correspondence study* (pp. 1–35). Dubuque, IA: Kendall/Hunt.

Watkins, R., & Kaufman, R. (2003). Strategic planning for distance education. In M. G. Moore & W. G. Anderson (Eds.), *Handbook of distance education* (pp. 507–517). Mahwah, NJ: Erlbaum.

Western Cooperative for Educational Telecommunications (WCET). (2000, November). *Guide to developing online services* (Putting Principles into Practice: Promoting Effective Support Services for Students in Distance Education Programs Report). Boulder, CO: Krauth, Barbara & Carbajal, Jennifer. Retrieved December 30, 2004, from http://www.wcet.info/resources/publications/guide1003/guide.pdf

Western Cooperative for Educational Telecommunications (WCET). (2001). *Best practices for electronically offered degree and certificate programs.* Washington, DC: Council for Regional Accrediting Commissions. Available from http://www.wcet.info/resources/accreditation/Accrediting%20-%20Best%20Practices.pdf

Western Cooperative for Educational Telecommunications (WCET). (2003). *Beyond the administrative core: Creating web-based student services for online learners* (Learning Anytime Anywhere Project [LAAP]). Boulder, CO: Shea & Armitage. Retrieved October 31, 2004, from http://www.wcet.info/projects/laap/guidelines/index.asp

White, K. W., & Weight, B. H. (2000). *The online teaching guide.* Boston: Allyn & Bacon.

Wikipedia. (n.d.) Retrieved January 5, 2005, from http://en.wikipedia.org/wiki/Open_source

Wiley, D. A. (2002). Connecting learning objects to instructional design theory: A definition, a metaphor, and a taxonomy. In D. A. Wiley (Ed.), *The instructional use of learning objects* (pp. 1–23). Bloomington, IN: Agency for Instructional Technology and Association for Educational Communications & Technology.

Willis, B. (1993). *Distance education: A practical guide*. Englewood Cliffs, NJ: Educational Technology.

Willis, B. (1994). Enhancing faculty effectiveness in distance education. In B. Willis (Ed.), *Distance education: Strategies and tools* (pp. 277–290). Englewood Cliffs, NJ: Educational Technology.

Wilson, C. (2001). Faculty attitudes about distance learning. *EDUCAUSE Quarterly, 24*(2), 70–71.

Wohler, K. (2004). *Copyright primer for online education: Copyright guidelines for online faculty at Washburn University*. Retrieved January 31, 2005, from http://www.washburn.edu/copyright/faculty/copyrightprimer.html#dmca

Wolcott, L. L. (2003). Dynamics of faculty participation in distance education: Motivations, incentives, and rewards. In M. G. Moore & W. G. Anderson (Eds.), *Handbook of distance education* (pp. 549–566). Mahwah, NJ: Erlbaum.

Yeung, D. (2002). Toward an effective quality assurance model. *Online Journal of Distance Learning Administration, 5*(2) [Online serial]. Available from http://www.westga.edu/~distance/ojdla/summer52/yeung52.htm

Young, J. R. (2002a, April 19). Pricing shifts by Blackboard and WebCT cost some colleges much more. *Chronicle of Higher Education, 48*(38), A35.

Young, J. R. (2002b, May 31). The 24-hour professor. *Chronicle of Higher Education, 48*(32), A31.

Young, J. R. (2004, July 23). Universities offer homegrown course software. *Chronicle of Higher Education, 50*(46), A27.

Zyman, S. (1999). *The end of marketing as we know it*. New York: HarperCollins.

INDEX

Printed in the United States
76268LV00001B/199-216